T0318312

This is a great introduction to digital marketing, which gets students up-to-speed in an easily digestible way. It covers some of the key areas of digital marketing communications, such as SEO, search engine advertising, email, etc. I highly recommend this book if you want something that explains key concepts in a clear and easy way, without the jargon.

—Tanya Hemphill, Senior Lecturer in Strategic &
Digital Marketing at Manchester Metropolitan
University, UK

Absolute Essentials of Digital Marketing

This short form textbook provides readers with a comprehensive yet concise overview of the fundamentals of Digital Marketing.

The author, a well-renowned teacher and writer on the subject, presents a concise and clear structure that works step by step through each of the core aspects of the subject, including SEO, metrics and analytics, web development, e-commerce, social media and digital marketing strategy.

Presented in nine chapters to suit delivery periods at both undergraduate and postgraduate levels, this book can be used either as a core text that gives tutors a sound platform on which to structure a module on digital marketing or as supporting text where digital marketing is an element of a module with a broader scope, such as strategic marketing.

Pedagogical features include an essential summary paragraph at the start of each chapter, focused references and further reading. There is also online teaching and learning support for both in-class and digital delivery, including suggested case studies, chapter questions and other activities.

Alan Charlesworth has been involved in what is now commonly referred to as 'digital marketing' in either practical, training, research, advisory, consultancy or academic roles since 1996.

Absolute Essentials of Business and Economics

Textbooks are an extraordinarily useful tool for students and teachers, as is demonstrated by their continued use in the classroom and online. Successful textbooks run into multiple editions, and in endeavouring to keep up with developments in the field, it can be difficult to avoid increasing length and complexity.

This series of shortform textbooks offers a range of books which zero-in on the absolute essentials. In focusing on only the core elements of each sub-discipline, the books provide a useful alternative or supplement to traditional textbooks.

Titles in this series include:

Absolute Essentials of Digital Marketing
Alan Charlesworth

Absolute Essentials of International Business
Alan Sitkin & Karine Mangion

Absolute Essentials of Project Management
Paul Roberts

Absolute Essentials of Business Behavioural Ethics
Nina Seppala

Absolute Essentials of Corporate Governance
Stephen Bloomfield

Absolute Essentials of Business Ethics
Peter A. Stanwick & Sarah D. Stanwick

For more information about this series, please visit: www.routledge.com/Absolute-Essentials-of-Business-and-Economics/book-series/ABSOLUTE

Absolute Essentials
of Digital Marketing

Alan Charlesworth

Routledge
Taylor & Francis Group

LONDON AND NEW YORK

First published 2021
by Routledge
2 Park Square, Milton Park, Abingdon, Oxon OX14 4RN

and by Routledge
52 Vanderbilt Avenue, New York, NY 10017

Routledge is an imprint of the Taylor & Francis Group, an informa business

© 2021 Alan Charlesworth

The right of Alan Charlesworth to be identified as author of this work
has been asserted by him in accordance with sections 77 and 78 of the
Copyright, Designs and Patents Act 1988.

British Library Cataloguing-in-Publication Data
A catalogue record for this book is available from the British Library

Library of Congress Cataloging-in-Publication Data
Names: Charlesworth, Alan, 1956– author.
Title: Absolute essentials of digital marketing /
Alan Charlesworth.
Description: New York : Routledge, 2020. |
Series: Absolute essentials of business and economics |
Includes bibliographical references and index.
Identifiers: LCCN 2020022712 (print) | LCCN 2020022713 (ebook) |
ISBN 9780367859206 (hardback) | ISBN 9781003015789 (ebook)
Subjects: LCSH: Internet marketing.
Classification: LCC HF5415.1265 C486 2020 (print) |
LCC HF5415.1265 (ebook) | DDC 658.8/72—dc23
LC record available at https://lccn.loc.gov/2020022712
LC ebook record available at https://lccn.loc.gov/2020022713

ISBN: 978-0-367-85920-6 (hbk)
ISBN: 978-0-367-61116-3 (pbk)
ISBN: 978-1-003-01578-9 (ebk)

Typeset in Times New Roman
by codeMantra

Visit the eResources: www.AlanCharlesworth.com/AEDM

This one's for Gavin … for helping to keep me sane over the years

Contents

Contents

Figures

Preface

This is a book on marketing. A book on marketing that focuses on the role that digital technology – concentrating on the Internet – *can* play in contemporary marketing.

In the same way that (for example) pricing and promotion are part of marketing, digital marketing is not a discipline in its own right; it is an element of marketing that can be used at both tactical and strategic levels.

Digital marketing is not compulsory in *effective* modern marketing. It is one of the tools in the marketing tool box – and in the same way that a hammer should not be used to remove a screw, digital marketing should be used only when it is appropriate to the customer, product and organization. In some circumstances *digital* will be essential; in some, useful; in others, totally inappropriate. The various elements of digital marketing – as covered in the chapters of this book – are *parts* of the marketing mix; they are not tactics and strategies to be used in isolation.

This book, therefore, should be used as *part of* a study of marketing – as a module, for example – not as a book that represents the *whole* of marketing.

Its purpose is not to evangelise *digital* marketing as 20th-century marketing. It *pragmatically* covers the various elements of digital marketing; how they are best practiced – their advantages and flaws – and their role in the marketing mix as part of the organization's strategic marketing efforts.

This book – hopefully – makes clear that *some* aspects of digital marketing are massively effective for the marketing of *some* organizations, *some* brands and *some* products. For others it is not so effective – and for others it is a complete waste of time, effort and resources. In essence, the contents of this book will help readers recognize which elements of digital marketing are *right* for a specific organization, brand or product ... and which are *wrong*. As business and economics academic, theorist and author Michael Porter famously said: 'The essence of strategy is choosing what *not* to do.' He makes a very valid point.

Acknowledgements

All at Routledge who helped make this publication possible.

Mat Bennett of OKO Ad Management who helped me get my head around programmatic advertising.

Andrew Hood of Lynchpin who helped me get to grips with some of the analytics stuff.

1 The digital marketing landscape

Essential summary

The opening chapter of this book introduces readers to some of the issues that are outside the various subjects covered in subsequent chapters, but are relevant to them all. First, the question of 'what is digital marketing' is addressed before readers are reminded that *digital* is not the only option open to marketers when deciding tactics or strategies. The thorny issue of there being a lot of non-marketers in digital marketing is then addressed. Relevant to business decisions of all kinds is whether tasks should be undertaken in-house or outsourced – the same is true of digital marketing. The next section considers the fads, trends and the occasional sustainable models that digital marketing is plagued or blessed with – depending on your point of view. Things that have stood the test of time include reviews and ratings, affiliate marketing, mobile applications, gaming and personalization. Still waiting for their big break in marketing are virtual and augmented reality whilst the jury is still out on viral marketing, influencers, content marketing and direct to consumer. A quick look at the so-called *big data* leads into the final subject of the chapter – privacy and trust.

What is digital marketing?

Defining *digital marketing* is not quite so straightforward as this characterization suggests, however. A clear, if simplistic, description that few could argue with is – *Marketing using digital technology*. However, it is the norm that *digital marketing* is used to describe only marketing on the Internet – ignoring that digital technology is used in just about every aspect of *non*-Internet marketing. The author of this book stands firmly in the *'digital marketing is marketing'* camp – or at least that it is an element of marketing. In marketing terms, digital options are part of the marketing mix.

> The author has spent the last 25 years or so asking the question – *has digital brought anything to marketing that is new to marketing?* and is yet to hear a *valid* positive response. Faster, more efficient, cost-saving ways of doing old things – certainly. But nothing *new*.

Digital isn't the only option

Digital technology has revolutionized *some* industries in ways unimaginable before the Internet came along – who books a hotel or flight anywhere other than online these days, for example? Similarly, for some products and services, the web plays an essential part in consumers' purchase decision making process. However, marketers must always be aware that *digital* is just one element of the marketing mix. For many products, putting them in the right place at the right time at the right price is sufficient for customers to buy them – this applies to the vast majority of retail products. For most B2B products digital has little role to play in their marketing. As with all marketing mix decisions, some elements are right for some products – but all are never right for all products. The job of the marketer is to identify which the elements of marketing are most suitable to the product or service they are marketing – and which are not. As Michael Porter famously said; 'The essence of strategy is choosing what *not* to do'.

Non-marketers in digital marketing

Since the onset of online marketing (generally agreed to be around 1994) there has always been a variance between marketers and IT staff/ computer scientists. To be successful in the digital environment there needs to be cohesion – teamwork – between the two skill sets. However, the technical nature of some aspects of digital marketing has led to those roles being taken by workers from computer scientist backgrounds – so creating a situation where there are a lot of people working as *digital marketers* who do not know even the fundamentals of marketing. These people may well be good, excellent even, at one aspect of digital marketing, but they do not appreciate how that element is – or should be – an integral part of a wider on- and offline strategies.

And the situation is getting worse because some of these non-marketers are being promoted to the positions of *digital managers* or even *marketing managers*. That's a situation that's unlikely to end happily for everyone involved. As Seth Godin said in his influential book, Meatball Sundae (2007): 'New marketing isn't about technology any more than fast food (and the drive-through window) is about cars'. That said, marketers must accept that too many of their numbers have shown little enthusiasm for learning the *very* basics of digital technology.

Marketing experts?

When a practicing digital marketer published a blog article titled *24 Marketers You Should Follow on Twitter*, outspoken and influential marketer, Mark Ritson took a look at the background of the 24 named *marketers*. He found that only four had any formal marketing training or education. Ritson's subsequent article in marketingweek.com caused something of a furore amongst the non-marketing marketers – but then it would, wouldn't it?

In-house or outsource?

A subject that reoccurs throughout the book because it is relevant to every subject is whether the organization can complete the task in-house or whether it needs to be outsourced to another businesses or individuals that specializes in that particular task. Such is the nature of digital marketing which has a number of *specialized* tasks that it is not uncommon for work to be outsourced to specialist agencies or personnel. Indeed, every subject area in this book has specialists who will undertake the work for organizations be they micro, small, large or global. The early days of marketing on the Internet saw just about every task being outsourced to people who knew what they were doing in this new discipline. However, as time has passed, these *specialist* skills have become more accessible to marketing staff – many of the people will be reading this book in order to gain at least the basics of the skills. An obvious issue is those subjects which require *technical* expertise. However, developments in software have resulted in that technical expertise being *relatively* easily gained by users who have not studied computer science. For the newcomer to digital marketing a clue to how common outsourcing is in various subjects is to look at how many agencies exist on the subject. A quick search on Google will show a multitude of digital advertising agencies, web design agencies and search engine optimization agencies. If they exist, then it is reasonable to assume that there is a demand for their skills.

Fads, trends and the occasional sustainable model

Since the birth of marketing on the Internet, *digital* has been home to a whole host of new ideas, models and concepts, most sporting an acronym or label to show how *trendy* they are. Some have stood the test of time; others never got off the ground. Most cross over the various elements of digital marketing and so some of the best known are included here.

What people do online

Research by Perrin (2020), on behalf of eMarketer, investigated selected activities undertaken by Internet users in the US showed that one of the original applications of the Internet – email – still holds top spot despite a plethora of newer, and trendier, applications since that time. Equally interesting to digital marketers is that search comes in at number two (Figure 1.1).

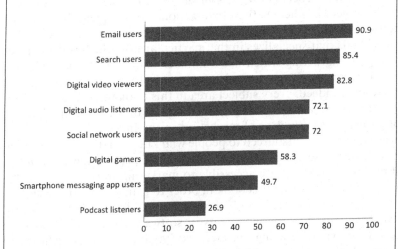

Figure 1.1 User participation in digital activities.

Reviews and ratings

Arguably, the aspect of the Internet that has had the biggest impact on business is the ability of customers to give their opinions of products and services to thousands – millions even – of total strangers. The impact of reviews on consumers is that as it is now more difficult to sell shoddy products or services, their quality has improved. Nowhere is this more in evidence than the holiday accommodation industry. Essentially, provide a poor service and get low ratings – and your bookings drop. However, the validity and authenticity of *some* reviews are now commonly questioned. A professional or serious hobby chef commenting on kitchen knives, for example, might be taken as valid advice from someone who *should* know what they are talking about. However, that requests for product reviews have become the default action for many sellers has resulted in the practice being diluted. Furthermore, public scepticism has been increased by reports of organizations *doctoring* reviews of their products or services. Worse still is another issue – the fake review. Long thought by many *insiders* to be commonplace in some industries and online platforms the practice has now been industrialised by false review providers.

Personalization

The term *personalization* describes the models, concepts and actions that meet the philosophy of the concept that each customer – be that an individual or organization – can receive a marketing message that is bespoke to that individual or organization. That is, the marketing is *personalized* to him, her or it (an organization) rather than being *broadcast* to a wide audience – some of who will have no interest in that message. Within the field of digital marketing personalization can be applied to websites, email, advertising and search engine optimization. It can include recommendations, promotions and pricing, and is made possible by a combination of digital metrics and analytics (which are covered in the last chapter). Personalization is, in effect, the concept of *segmentation, targeting and positioning* (STP). However, whilst in the traditional application of the model it is difficult to narrow the constituent parts to specific individuals, the Internet, mobile technology and the availability of data has made it possible – theoretically – for segments of *one* to be targeted.

Viral marketing

The concept of *viral marketing* is based on the traditional practice of word-of-mouth marketing (also known as *referral marketing* and *network marketing*) – an oral, person-to-person communication between a receiver and a communicator regarding a brand, a product or a service (Arndt, 1967). In essence, viral marketing describes any marketing strategy or tactic that encourages individuals to pass on *promotional* message to others. Successful execution means the message's exposure grows exponentially – like a virus. The contribution made by digital media is that once the word is out, it can get around faster than ever before. There are, however, a couple of significant – and associated – problems with the ubiquitous use of the term *viral marketing*. First is the general public and news media's common usage of the term *gone viral* which is not associated with marketing, for example, a funny video of someone doing something foolish. Second, there is the common misunderstanding and/or misinterpretation of what viral marketing actually is. If a customer buys a product, likes it and then tells her friends how good it is that is not viral (or word-of-mouth) marketing, it is the social phenomenon of people spreading something from person to person. For it to be marketing it has to be a planned and structured part of an organization's promotional mix – where the customer is *encouraged* to pass on the message, usually with the offer of some kind of reward.

Content marketing

Defined by the Content Marketing Institute as: 'a strategic marketing approach focused on creating and distributing valuable, relevant, and consistent content to attract and retain a clearly defined audience — and, ultimately, to drive profitable customer action', this is another contemporary marketing tactic and strategy that has seen a re-birth in the digital age. Whilst content can simply be the *non-sales* content of a website (e.g. describing how products can be used – which is good practice anyway) *strategic* content marketing would include the specific development of content to be published in such formats as: social media (e.g. tweets, Facebook entries), blogs, articles, white papers, case studies, white papers, research reports, guides, webinars, shared documents, podcasts, Q+A pages, videos, forums, infographics and PR. It is because all of this content – which is not necessarily hosted on the organization's website – can bring visitors and links into the site that it is sometimes referred to as *inbound marketing*. The objectives of content marketing can include: increased web traffic, direct sales, up-selling/cross-selling, customer retention, brand awareness, brand loyalty, customer acquisition, engagement, customer relations, lead generation or thought leadership and it is equally valid in both

B2B and B2C markets. However, it is worth mentioning that an important aspect of search engine optimization is to create links into the site and one way of achieving this is to have *content* published on a variety of websites and for that content to include a link to the organization's website. It is for this reason that it is not unusual for some practitioners and industry commentators to refer to content marketing as *link building* – ignoring the other potential objectives as listed above.

Influencers

Marketers have always been aware of *influencers* – in the loyalty ladder model, the advocate (influencer) sits at the top – and tells friends/colleagues about product *organically;* that is as part of conversation, not for payment. Similarly, using celebrities to endorse products has always been commonplace. However, like most marketing practices, the concept was only *formalised* after its long-term practice – in this case by Katz and Lazarfeld in 1955. Traditional influencers were personalities chosen to promote (usually in adverts) particular products or brands – but they were, by necessity, famous people who commanded attention from the public and high fees from marketers. The link between product and celebrity may have been candid (an actor looking *cool* smoking a cigarette brand) or more tenuous – singer and actress Doris Day posing on an industrial road roller in an ad for the *International Harvester Company*, for example. Furthermore, being personalities in TV, radio or print made these offline influencers a kind of *elite*.

Perhaps *influenced* by non-marketers (as described early in the chapter) the term has strayed from its real meaning in recent times. The Merriam-Webster dictionary's definition of; *one who exerts influence: a person who inspires or guides the actions of others* gives focus to someone who has influence by way of personality or altruism. Although such people – or organizations – still exist, a *digital marketing* definition would be something like; a person who is paid by their sellers to show and describe products and services on social media, encouraging other people to buy them. However, there is another definition that is essential; in legal terms, that *encouragement* is a sponsored post, and so is deemed to be an advertisement and so must be identified as such – something that escapes many of the *influenced*.

Traditional influencers continue to exist, particularly from the fields of sports or entertainment, with many using their *authority* in altruistic ways – promoting health issues or condemning racism, for example. Others are more mercenary, using their fame to gain further notoriety – and income – as digital influencers. However, digital marketers soon realized that this new wave of online influencers were not necessarily famous personalities, and so could be *hired* for much lower fees – often simply the products they were being asked to endorse. However, such is the nature of 21st-century celebrity status that some influencers have become famous for being influencers – and these command significant amounts of money to endorse a product (though see Chapter 8 where the issue of fake followers is addressed).

Although the use of *digital* influencers can be effective, this is limited to certain markets. Perhaps because females represent 87 per cent of all influencers (according to research published in 2020 by IZEA who *claim* to have created the modern influencer marketing industry in 2006) clothes and cosmetics are examples of where influencer marketing works – their effectiveness is other industries is questionable. Furthermore, as is the case with all social media marketing, calculating ROI can be difficult – *engagement* does not necessarily translate into purchases. There are also the issues of the quality of the influencer's followers (real or fake?) and that influencers' misdemeanours can result in them going from hero to zero overnight. When mattress company Casper filing for IPO it listed influencers among the risk factors that could give investors sleepless nights.

However, perhaps the biggest threat comes from the legal profession. By law, an influencer's comments are an advert and so must be clearly labelled as such – something that has not been vigorously monitored. However, February 2020 saw the US Federal Trade Commission (FTC) introduce its Endorsement Guides (for *endorsement*, read *influence*) which looks to punish the influencers personally as well as the organizations employing them. Not only might this serve to moderate the practice, but having an influencer start their promo video with; 'I've been paid to say that …' might diminish its effectiveness as marketing tool.

Virtual influence

There are influencers out there who will do and say anything a brand tells them to – and they're guaranteed not to act or speak out of place. Welcome to the world of the *virtual* influencer – a software-driven entity that presents itself as a real person. And apparently – despite the fact that the influencer is, in effect, a sales*person* for the products it endorses – some customers are actually *influenced* by them.

Affiliate marketing

Affiliate programmes have long been an *offline* business model in their own right; however, as the book is about using the Internet as a medium for marketing, this section considers only the use of affiliates as a means of digitally marketing a product. Digital affiliate programmes are a form of performance-based marketing where a commission is paid only if a sale is completed. Because multiple affiliate programmes can function on multiple websites, the notion of selling things through the practice has been dubbed *affiliate marketing*. As far as the user is concerned, an affiliate link is an *advert* and it is difficult for the uninitiated to tell the difference. Similarly, the buyer might simply perceive the affiliate website as being a retail site. Accurate figures are difficult – if not impossible – to determine, but it is believed that around 10 per cent of all online sales involve affiliate marketing, with some estimates for specific industries (such as online gambling) rising as high as 20 per cent. For the business promoting goods through affiliate networks the major advantage is that not only is their reach into different markets increased, but the affiliated website(s) effectively *sell* the product for them. If done well, affiliate marketing can provide a cost-effective and highly measurable way to acquire customers and grow sales.

Direct to consumer (DTC)

In the mid-1990s predictions were that the Internet would see all shops closed by the turn of the new century. This has, obviously, not proved to be the case, with the reason being found in the concept of the *chain* (or *channel*) *of distribution*. This is where groups of manufacturers supply retailers who, in turn, offer buyers a whole range of products under one roof. Rarely are products sold directly from the manufacturer to the end user who is unwilling to spend several hours ordering a tin of soup from Heinz.com, bread from Warburtons.co.uk, carrots from somefarmsomewhere.co.uk and so on and so on. However, for some manufacturers, it can make sense and we are now seeing some manufacturers selling direct to consumers. This being the case – and here lays the attraction of DTC – as there is no middleman to take their slice of any income, there is more profit to be made. The DTC concept is applied to manufacturers whose sales are online only. The most successful of these invariably manufacture and sell few, or even single, products – making sales, marketing and distribution less complex. A further opportunity is for manufacturers to sell some – or even just one – of their products direct-to-consumers. This is particularly the case if the product is fixed (i.e. one size/colour/etc.) and small enough to be delivered through a letterbox. To date, however, the concept has seen little significant success.

Gaming

Although the potential of gaming as a vehicle for marketing has been around for some time, interest in it has increased driven by two significant factors: (1) the rise and popularity of Massive Multiplayer Online collaborative games (MMOs), and (2) the phenomenon of eSports competitions that attract millions of spectators both online and offline. Although sponsoring eSports events or star players is an option for marketers, realistically that is limited to major brands. More common is advertising within mobile gaming apps, with display, native, rich media and video ads all being available within online gaming apps. A further consideration is that the top gamers and those who comment on the *industry* (e.g. bloggers) are also ideal candidates for hire as *influencers* who can reach a number of targeted segments.

Mobile applications

If ever there was a subject to exemplify the advances in, and acceptance of, technology it is in the development and adoption of mobile devices that can access the Internet. Indeed, in a very short space of time the smartphone has gone from the *latest gizmo* to *must have accessory* to *can't live without*. Because consumers can access the web and share information on the go, the subject is inherent to all aspects of digital marketing. Such is the impact of the *always-connected* customer on the organization that it is their expectation that all tasks should be easily achievable from a mobile device. Various sources suggest that around 50 per cent of Internet access is on mobile devices, though *mobile minutes* are higher than this as they include the use of apps and reading, watching or listening to downloaded material.

Virtual and augmented reality

According to industry website augment.com; 'virtual reality (VR) offers a digital recreation of a real life setting, while augmented reality (AR) delivers virtual elements as an overlay to the real world'. In further differentiating the two, the site goes on to say that 'VR is usually delivered to the user through a head-mounted, or hand-held controller. This equipment connects people to the virtual reality, and allows them to control and navigate their actions in an environment meant to simulate the real world', whilst 'AR is being used more and more in mobile devices such as laptops, smart phones and tablets to change how the real world and digital images, graphics intersect and interact'. Both technologies have numerous applications in the likes of entertainment, medicine and training but their marketing applications are limited – predominantly to do with novelty, which raises the question of whether the technology offers any real value for consumers and marketers.

Big data

Something of a misnomer as there is no distinction as to when data transforms into *big* data, this refers to the collection of data from and about everything internal and external to the organization and the interpretation of that data to help make the business run more efficiently and improve customer service. It facilitates the ability to track customers and their communications across every channel which can help measure and manage the *customer experience* – the sum of all the experiences a customer has with a business. Not all commentators are positive, however. Key issues raised with regard to big data's value to the organization include:

- The data itself is not so important as its analysis and ability to use that analysis in decision making.
- Mathematical algorithms produce data in abundance on what has happened – or *is* happening – but they have difficulty answering the question of *why* things are happening. That is where the analytics come in.
- Shouldn't we first learn to maximize value from *smaller* data before going big?
- Is any of the data being used to the detriment of the individuals that data is about?

Artificial intelligence (AI)

According to Russell and Norvig (2003), 'the term *artificial intelligence* is applied when a machine mimics *cognitive* functions that humans associate with other human minds, such as *learning* and *problem solving*'. Note that *machine learning* is not AI – the latter is an *extension* of the former.

Although still something of a *buzz* phrase, not only has the concept been a reality for some time, but such are the advances in technology that actions once classed as AI are now demoted to being the mundane – for example, the character recognition used in scanning documents and voice recognition software such as Apple's Siri and Amazon's Alexa. Other examples include:

- Personalization of marketing messages.
- Google has been using its *RankBrain*, an AI system, in its advertising since late 2015 (though not for organic search which is deemed too subjective for machine learning/AI).
- Chatbots.
- Dynamic pricing.
- Product recommendations.
- Data analysis.

However, such is the hype for AI that many things described as AI are in reality (only) algorithms that run automatic processes through machine learning and uses robotics and rules-based systems to predict outcomes. Ultimately, like *big data*, AI is something that marketers will use unknowingly as an integral part of a tool or application – the outcome being far more important than the technology that helps achieve it.

Privacy and trust

It is worth starting this section by reminding readers that data – their data – is a commodity that can be sold by those who collect and analyze it to third parties who are then free to use it as they wish. This has always been a pre-Internet business model, but the ease of collection and analyze facilitated by digital technology has increased disproportionately the potential financial benefits of the model. Indeed, for many businesses, their brand – and stock exchange – value is built around the data it possesses on its customers and uses and its ability to gather more. Zhou and Li (2014) describe the concept of *privacy concerns* as referring to individuals' beliefs about the risks and potential negative consequences associated with sharing information. However, this does not address people's actions as a result of those potential negative consequences which are that as the knowledge of the causes of these consequences has become more common, not only have the concerns increased, but so too have people's actions to address them – a balancing act dubbed the *privacy paradox*. Essentially, this is a trade-off between giving organizations personal data and the benefits gained from allowing those organizations to use it.

At the core of people's privacy is the *digital footprint* that Internet users leave as they wander around the web. Every click; every web page they visit; every ad they are exposed to; every ad they click on; every search they conduct; every email they are sent, receive, open, delete or reply to; every visit to a social media platform; every tweet they receive; every comment they make on a feedback form; everything they buy; everything they nearly buy; everything they look at but don't buy; where in the world they are when they do these things (via their smartphone's GPS); when they do all of these things – minute, hour, day, month and year; how often they do these things; what device(s) they use to do these things is recorded ... and much more.

Is help at hand?

May 2018 saw the first major initiative with regard to data protection – the *General Data Protection Regulation (GDPR)* which had the aim of protecting all EU citizens from privacy and data breaches. It applies to all companies processing the personal data of data subjects residing in the Union, regardless of the company's location.

The United States followed suit on January 1, 2020 with the California Consumer Privacy Act (CCPA) applies to any business, including any for-profit entity that collects consumers' personal data, which does business in California and satisfies at least one of certain thresholds, including:

- Has annual gross revenues in excess of $25 million;
- Buys or sells the personal information of 50,000 or more consumers or households; or
- Earns more than half of its annual revenue from selling consumers' personal information.

Furthermore, the first two months of 2020 saw announcements that:

- The UK's regulator Ofcom was to have more authority over UK social media including new powers for the media watchdog to force social media firms to act over harmful content.
- Facebook will pay Reuters to fact-check *deepfake* videos and more in the fight against misinformation on the social media platform.
- Google is going to block cookies – a source of third-data about used by programmatic advertising – on its Chrome browser from early 2022.

Only time will tell if this is the start of users retaining their privacy and trusting organization's to use their personal data responsibly – but with individuals' data being a valuable commodity, that does not seem too likely.

Digital marketing objectives

Without specific objectives the likelihood of any venture succeeding diminishes significantly as the organization cannot (1) determine whether the online activity has been successful, or (2) assess the return on investment (ROI) for any online operations. To be successful, any organization needs to have a plan that looks further to the future than next week's sales – with some aspects of business requiring longer term planning: *strategic* planning. Finance is the obvious example, something that is generally planned and assessed on at least an annual basis. Similarly, production requires raw materials to be ordered and shipped long before the production process starts. Planning that looks further forward is deemed to be *strategic* in nature.

Strategic digital objectives

Although the dynamic nature of the digital environment makes for a reasonable argument that it is impossible to plan *strategically*, long-term objectives are necessary so that the various elements of digital marketing, particularly where aspects might be managed and/or delivered by different departments need to have their operations coordinated to be most effective. It is also the case that some elements of digital marketing are more suited to one objective or another. Several of these are overt – network adverts being more suited to branding, for example – with other elements being intrinsic to the objectives such as prominent calls-to-action on e-commerce sites.

There are three potential key objectives to any digital marketing endeavours which align closely with offline marketing objectives. They are:

1   Brand development – where any online presence compliments and enhances the branding efforts of the organization.
2   Revenue/income generation – where the online presence acts as a *commerce* or *acquisition* channel in order to increase revenue into the organization by direct sales or lead generation.
3   Customer care/service/support – where the web is used to enhance the service and support offered to customers.

Although having a single objective that covers all aspects of digital marketing is feasible, it could be that the overall objective is *primary* rather than *exclusive*. Therefore, for clarity in identifying *strategic* online objectives, it is necessary to identify the *primary* objective, expressed as a percentage. For example; an offline-only retailer might have a primary objective of customer care (on social media) and allocate 75 per cent of its resources to it, with only a basic corporate site (10 per cent) and some network advertising (15 per cent) for branding. An offline-only white goods manufacturer, however, might have a key objective of branding (90 per cent), customer care at 10 per cent and zero to online sales. Whilst it may be possible to have separate *strategic* objectives for different elements of digital marketing, this is likely to result in a fragmented overall strategy and so is best left to operational objectives.

Operational digital objectives

These are – effectively – sub-sections of strategic objectives that are applied to individual campaigns or initiatives that can be measured by metrics such as key performance indicators (KPIs) in a way that is impossible for long-term strategic objectives. Consider, for example, an online objective of income generation via direct sales – a strategy that is to be achieved over a period of years. This means that the outcome cannot be measured until the end of that period, with sales dipping, peaking and remaining constant within that phase of time – increased sales at Christmas, for example. Operational objectives on the other hand can use short-term models of measurement such as the SMART mnemonic. An advertising campaign aimed at driving customers to the website with the intention that they buy a promoted product (so helping meet the strategic sales objective) can be:

- Specific – to sell x units of the product (this based on a percentage increase over previous sales).
- Measurable – has the sales target been met, exceeded or not met, and by what percentage or amount.
- Achievable – can the organization meet the target, this would also include such issues as availability and logistics.
- Realistic – based on prior sales, the sales target must be one that is practically able to be met.
- Time-bound – the advertising campaign will run for two weeks with the promotion continuing for another two weeks after that.

It is also possible that operational objectives can supplement second-ary as well as strategic key objectives – a short-term PR campaign to raise the brand profile, for example, might help raise sales over the longer, strategic period. It is also the case that in a dynamic digital environment, being able to react to changes in technology, the market and customer expectations by adjusting tactics is essential whilst still pursuing the overall key objective in a holistic manner. However, a ca-veat is that in constantly focusing on changing tactics, marketers *must not* lose sight of the key objective.

A footnote to this section is that although *digital* might have its own strategic and operational objectives, they must be part of the organi-zation's overall marketing and business objectives. Indeed, online ob-jectives are frequently dictated by offline tactics or the organization's corporate strategy.

Further reading

For additional content and links to articles and stories that supplement this chapter, go to its web page on www.AlanCharlesworth.com/AEDM.

References

Arndt, J. (1967) *Word of Mouth Advertising. A Review of the Literature.* Adver-tising Research Foundation, New York.
Godin, S. (2007) *Meatball Sundae.* Piatkus.

Perrin, N. (2020) Search in 2020. eMarketer. Available at: https://www.emarketer.com/content/mobile-search-ad-performance-plays-catch-up.

Russell, S. and Norvig, P. (2003) *Artificial Intelligence: A Modern Approach.* Pearson.

Zhou, T. and Li, H. (2014) *Understanding Mobile SNS Continuance Usage in China from the Perspectives of Social Influence and Privacy Concern.* Computers in Human Behaviour, Volume 37, pp. 283–289.

2 Search engine optimization

Essential summary

This chapter begins by differentiating organic and paid search (advertising) before explaining what search engine optimization (SEO) entails and its importance to the organization. This takes readers into the main body of this chapter: how search engines work. A brief description of the zero-click phenomenon before the crucial issue of keywords is discussed along with how search engines distinguish intent and location to deliver personalized searches. Actual optimization is addressed in two parts: first, on-site optimization of the web page content and source code and then off-site optimization. Third-party SERP ranking using directories and third-party websites concludes this chapter.

Organic vs paid search

An issue that will resurface in subsequent chapters is that of the definitions for some of the subject areas. Most significant is the author's long-held belief that advertising online is a subject, discipline and skill in its own right. It is, therefore covered in Chapter 7 where all aspects and options of advertising on the Internet are addressed. This chapter covers all aspects of search engine optimization (SEO), that is getting (or trying to get) a website (or individual page) high on the *organic* – or *natural* – search engine results page (SERP) for specific searches by users. When a website is included on an organic SERP list the search engine makes no charge – the listing is free. However, also on (most) SERPs are ads for which the advertisers have paid a fee to have them listed (hence the practice sometimes being known as *paid search*). Getting an effective ad onto the SERP requires a completely different skill set than achieving a high organic listing. It is common for organic and ad listings to be considered to be described as search engine *marketing* (SEM). This is fine as long as the organization, team or individual recognizes that SEM consists of the two disparate elements.

What is SEO?

Search engines follow the business model in which a service is provided that attracts users to a website – and sells advertising on that site. To be successful in attracting users the search engine must satisfy the needs of its users. To satisfy them best, the search engine must respond to the users' searches with results – websites – that address the problem for which the searcher is seeking an answer. In essence, therefore, SEO is the practice of making a website attractive to a search engine by presenting its code and content in such a way that the search engine will assume that it will address a specific inquiry from a (human) searcher. For many, this aspect of digital marketing is both mysterious and somewhat mystifying, not least because (1) it is dependent on some extremely complicated mathematical algorithms, and (2) the term *search engine optimization* is something of a misnomer – suggesting that it is the search engines that are being optimized when it is actually the web pages that are optimized.

Google gets a lot of mentions in this chapter. There are several reasons for this, not least that:

- Although other search engines exist Google is by far the market leader.
- Google releases a lot of information and guidance for SEO on their engine.
- Most SEO research is conducted about/on Google.

Why is SEO important?

Since the birth of the commercial Internet, search engines have been seen as the portal – *front door* – to the Internet. The majority of people looking for a product or service start on a search engine (87 per cent according to Salesforce in 2018) – so if you wanted to sell anything you had to have a high ranking on the SERP. Although other methods of finding products or services are out there it is still search engines – predominantly Google, hence its prominence in this chapter – that bring the majority of potential customers to websites.

Users can arrive on a website by one of four means:

1   Search – the user clicks on an *organic* link on a search engine re-sults page.
2   Direct – the user types the web page's URL directly into their browser or from a bookmark.
3   Referral – the user clicks on a link on another website (including adverts)
4   Social – the user clicks on a link on a social media platform.

Extensive research by Amazon's @Alexa (2020) shown in Figure 2.1 emphasizes just how important SEO is to organizations that want customers to visit their website. If we add to this data that it is likely that many people who have bookmarked or remembered a website's URL originally found it via a search engine and the *search-derived* percentage moves along a bit further. Although social media is covered in Chapter 9, these statistics are a stark indication of its lack of effectiveness as a source of website traffic.

Results from a survey by BrightEdge Technologies (2019) are similar to research from other organizations, suggesting that over half of (53 per cent) of traffic to websites arrives via organic search engine

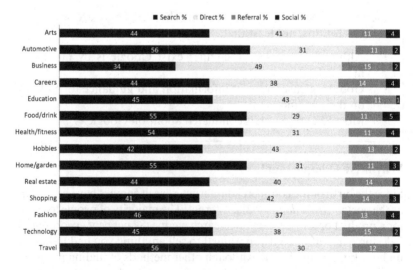

Figure 2.1 Website traffic sources (@Alexa, 2020).

results, with a further 15 per cent coming from SERP ads (paid search) – the *search* combination delivering significantly more traffic to websites than other channels, including social and display advertising. These statistics should come as no surprise if a study from Eli Schwartz (2018) of research specialists SurveyMonkey is taken into account. He found that when asked how they might seek out a needed product or service a visit to a search engine was the top response at 36 per cent. Social media trailed all other options at five per cent. And therein lays the reason why this book's examination of the various elements of digital marketing starts with *search engine optimization*. At the beginning of any organization's journey along the highway of digital marketing there is a key decision to make which will dictate the direction that journey takes. The issue to be addressed is this:

> Is the product or service one that people will seek or discover via a search engine – so inferring that in order for it to be successful in the marketplace it will be necessary for the product/service to be on the first page of the SERP for the appropriate keywords.

If the answer to this is *no*, then SEO is irrelevant to the organization and its marketing budget should be spent elsewhere. If the answer is *yes*, then existing circumstances will dictate which of two roads the digital marketing strategy will travel (Figure 2.2).

A final note for the digital marketer is that search engines are something of a law unto themselves, caring little for the businesses in

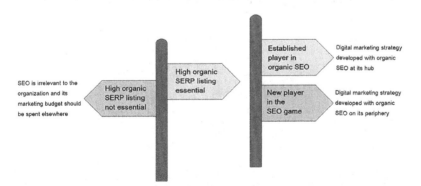

Figure 2.2 The route of any digital marketing strategy is determined by the organization's reliance on search engines to find new customers – that route being signposted by (a) how essential high SERP listings are and subsequently (b) whether or not the organization, brand or product has an existing SERP presence.

their listings (remember, their objective is to provide a service for the *searcher*, not those who want to be found). Therefore, any business – but particularly *pure-play* online traders – should be wary of total dependence of organic search engine listings for their online traffic. A simple change in a search engine's algorithm or increased SEO activity from a competitor could see a prized top organic listing disappear overnight – reducing new customers to zero. Naturally, paid advertising might take up some of the slack, but it is doubtful that referral numbers will be maintained.

How search engines work

The process starts with the search engine using *spiders* (or *bots*) that travel around the web gathering up data on websites that is then stored in vast indexes. It is from these indexes that search results are gleaned. The search engine uses the data to assesses each website's suitability in matching the search criteria (the algorithm), which it then presents as the results of its assessment (the SERP). The key – and secret – of the results is the *algorithm* used to calculate the rankings. Think of the algorithm as a jigsaw made up of lots of pieces with each representing a single element of the algorithm – Google is *said* to have around 200 factors in its algorithm – each of which is awarded *points* depending on how well they match the searcher's query. If a web page achieves a complete *picture* of the jigsaw it has the highest total of points total and so appears at the top of the SERP. The page with only one piece of the jigsaw is way down there on a SERP that no one ever looks at (Figure 2.3).

Figure 2.3 Effective SEO can be compared with building a jigsaw from all of the necessary elements of the search engine's algorithm.

Simple? Well, not quite. All pieces of a jigsaw are not *equal*, the straight edges are more important and the corners even more so. The same goes for the algorithm – the elements do not have equal weighting with some being deemed more important and so scoring more points. Worse still is that it is likely that a small number of the factors score more points than all the others combined. In other words, the SEO jigsaw maker is looking to fill the four corners before any other piece – and the four corners might be worth more points than a picture that has every piece in place except for the corners. The specifics of the various search engines' algorithms are, for obvious reasons, all closely guarded secrets. In the jigsaw analogy, the SEO is building the puzzle blindfold. Based on their experience, expertise and research, practitioners in search engine optimization *surmise* the key factors – the corners – and they may well be accurate with their deductions, but they're basically calculated guesses. But that is not the end of the SEO's problems. The search engines change their algorithms on a regular (some say daily) basis, adding or deleting factors and changing the weightings. So not only is our jigsaw maker blindfold, some of the pieces are being changed as they try to build the picture.

Sadly for the inexperienced optimizer, any attempt to try and fool the search engine with inappropriate actions (e.g. see keyword stuffing later in this chapter) results in points being deducted – so trying to force the wrong piece into a space in the jigsaw is not advised. Whilst the question of their weighting is important, it is the actual factors in the algorithm that take the concentration of the search engine optimizer – though naturally, if a specific factor is identified as having a significant weighting, it is common sense to make sure that factor is addressed correctly. For some factors of the algorithms, there is a certain level of agreement between the industry experts, and these can be divided into (1) the on-site placement of keywords, and (2) the off-site issues that can improve a site's SE popularity – these are addressed later in this chapter.

Zero-click

A phenomenon that has been building for a while are searches on Google that result in users being presented with the information they're looking for without clicking off the SERP – research from respected SEO expert, Rand Fishkin (2019) suggests that this accounts for around half of *all* searches (see Figure 2.2). Fortunately for SEOs, it would appear that Google has realized that raising this percentage still further would be counter-productive and seems to have held off

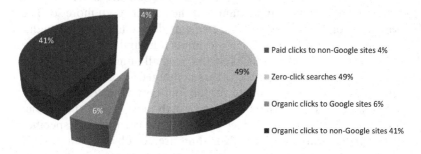

Figure 2.4 Where users click after searching on Google (Fishkin, 2019).

from increasing it still further. Note that this zero-click information might include businesses listed on Google My Business (GMB) – a free listing on Google that includes a description of the business, contact details and opening hours, but who do not have a website or Google's Home Hub which can feature such things as *How To* videos from websites or YouTube (Figure 2.4).

Furthermore, links to Google-owned sites from the SERP – if organic and ads are combined – represent around 10 per cent of all click throughs, so Google is actually sweeping up around 60 per cent of all searches. That leaves all the search engine optimizers fighting for less than half of all searches. However, all is not lost for organic search. As revealed in Figure 2.2 for every click on a paid result – *advert* – on a Google SERP, there are around 12 clicks to organic results.

Keywords

One of the corner pieces of the jigsaw is the characters typed into the search box by the searcher. For the sake of simplicity, throughout this book they will be referred to as *keywords*. However, it is common for the *keywords* to be called a *term* or *query*. However, before keywords can be included in website content, they must be identified. This can be (1) performed in-house (some are pretty obvious), (2) sought from customers (ask them) or (3) developed with the aid of technology (Google provide a record of what terms were used in searches where the searcher clicked through to the organization's site and keyword research tools are commonly available that will indicate what keywords are used in searches for certain products or services). Problems around keywords do not end with their selection, however – the level of competition in the market is also a consideration. If a product is represented by popular keywords, then its web page is competing with every other website that has been optimized for the same term. This is particularly true if the product or service has a generic identification – such as *smart phone* or *insurance*, for example.

The long tail

If the head represents the most commonly used search terms for a product, then one way of addressing the issue is to optimize for phrases searchers might use that are more specific to what is being sought. This is the so-called *long tail* of keywords. In his 2006 book, Chris Anderson uses the example of the long tail of music, where a shop would stock the 50 best-selling CDs (it was 2006, there was no digital downloads) – but buyers were looking to purchase thousands of CDs that were not in the top 50. Traditionally, these CDs – and before them, records – could be found in a bricks-and-mortar *niche* music shop. Anderson argued that the web replaced these shops and made finding back-catalogue music so much easier. The general concept for search engines is that *seasoned* users make specific searches. Rather than "hotel Porto" for example, a traveller might type in "hotel Porto 4 star swimming pool free WIFI parking restaurant balcony close to city centre" (note that the search engines ignore the niceties of grammar – generally searchers do so also). The long tail concept recognizes that not every hotel in Porto offers all of these requirements but one offering all of these services should be optimized for the keywords.

Intent

It has always been the case that – to a certain degree – the search engines could recognize searchers intent when they typed in a keyword or phrase; "emergency plumber", for example. However, technology has moved on. Led by Google's BERT (Bidirectional Encoder Representations from Transformers) – artificial intelligence-driven software that has a deeper sense of context in which language is used – so too has the search engines' ability to understand and interpret intent. This being the case, are keywords on the way out and *intent* the new kid on the block? As the experts – practitioners as well as representatives of various search engines – cannot agree, the answer is somewhere along the lines of; it would seem that it is likely that 2020 will see the search engines moving towards being primarily intent-based; but the days of the importance of keyword matching will never pass altogether. For the SEO community, this (probably) means a switch from current practices around keyword research and placement to those of intent. That said, certain words or phrases suggest, or intimate, intent – so perhaps we should be talking about *intent* keywords? An obvious example is that the search is *transactional* is if the searcher types the word *buy* in front of a product then they're likely to be looking for an outlet (online or offline) that sells them. However, a search for "what kind of washing machine is best for me?" is more *informational* in nature, and so the page on a retail website listing washing machines will not best serve their intent.

Andrei Broder's seminal paper *A taxonomy of web search* (2002) was so influential that his identification of three types of search is used by Google in how its algorithm *rates* human searchers (he also went on to work at the search giant).

- Informational (know) – looking for a specific fact or topic
- Navigational (go) – seeks to locate a specific website
- Transactional (do) – searching for information related to buying a particular product or service

It is estimated that around 80 per cent of searches are informational with the other two taking 10 per cent each.

Localization

A subject that has evolved along with the development of the search engines is that of serving searchers with results that are locally relevant to them – so-called *proximity* searches. Any searches that exhibit the appropriate *intent* will deliver a result that defaults to the search term ending with "near me". Indeed, the generation that has grown up with smartphones assume that they will be given local results at the top of the SERP. Furthermore, *near me* can be different for every search made by the same user. The searcher is no longer certain to be sitting in an office or house when seeking an outlet with a product in stock, they are *anywhere*. Localization impacts on keyword selection in a number of ways, not least that it can favour the smaller – local – business. The most obvious is in the address of the business, which will include region, city or district and so allows the search engine to pinpoint the businesses location on a map. For the national (or even global) organization having a web page *optimized* for every outlet can be problematic – though not impossible for the can-do company.

Personalized searches

Although it was always suspected by many practitioners and commentators that from its early days Google personalizing users' search results depending on each searcher's search history, the practice is now the norm. Indeed, there is a strong argument that personalization is now the *key* aspect of organic results – and it is something the marketer cannot influence (they are not even given this piece of the algorithm jigsaw). Rather than delivering the same results to everyone who searches on a specific term, personalized search considers the searcher's activity on the web; the websites they visit, search terms used, favourites in a browser, ads clicked on ... and so much more of the data the likes of Google collects on its users. Essentially, over the years Google has changed from being an *information* engine to a *knowledge* engine with the aim of understanding each user's intent for searching – and then providing the best answer it can on the first page of the search results. This knowledge aspect is emphasized in results of searches for well-indexed subjects, such as movies or countries, which feature a *knowledge panel* to the right of the main results.

On-site optimization

In essence, this task is all about placing the keywords and phrases within the web page. This can be in two elements of the website: (1) that which is visible to the human visitor – its *content*, and (2) that which is part of the source code of the page and so is visible only to the search engines.

Web page content

Also known as the *body* text – because it fits into the source code in the body command – this is the textual content of the website that the visitor has come to read. Some put forward the argument that this is the most important aspect of SEO, and there is some validity – and sense – in their line of reasoning, which is that if the search engine is looking to meet the needs of the searcher then the keywords that they use should be an inherent, *organic* aspect of the site's textual content. Furthermore, the way those keywords are included or presented on the page will help the search engine match the context of the search and intention of the searcher – section headers, for example. This is an example of why the non-advertising listings on a SERP are referred to as being *organic* or *natural*. If, for instance, a web page was about apples it would be strange if the word *apple* wasn't in both the title of the page and within proceeding content.

Voice search

Prompted by developments in technology, Internet-connected devices now come complete with a voice search facility. Such searches are on the increase – and so pages should be optimized for them. Although good content development will have already addressed this, the AI-supported personal assistants are more discerning than typed searches as spoken searches give the search engines more information to work with. This is because searchers do not simply insert truncated, verb-less key terms; they ask questions in the same way as they would to another human being. This helps the search engine to deliver fewer, but more specific, returns to voice searches.

Source code

The argument in favour of including keywords in a web page's source code is that it helps the search engine spider identify the page's subject. In reality, with a few exceptions – detailed below – search engine optimizers agree the practice has little purpose. That said, given that each entry takes only a few minutes, the investment is not extreme – and as all of the entries should correspond with the actual content of each page it does help encourage good practice in content development. It is also the case that some of these *meta tags* appear as the page description in SERPs and so are worthwhile for that reason. For example, a page's title tag is shown in blue as the *headline* of the SERP listing and so influence clickthrough rates (CTR). Research from Brian Dean of Backlinko (2019) found that titles that were a question have a 14.1 per cent higher CTR vs. pages that don't have a question in their title and URLs that contain a keyword have a 45 per cent higher click through rate compared to URLs that don't contain a keyword (the URL of the listed page is shown with the title text).

Brian Dean (2019) looked at the impact of organic SERP position on CTR. His findings included that:

1   The #1 result in Google's organic search results has an average CTR of 31.7 per cent, which is around ten times higher

than a page in the #10 spot – suggesting that Google users instinctively click on the first result in Google.

2 The CTR drops significantly after position #5. This might be because few users scroll down past the 5th result – which is likely to be *below the fold*.

3 The CTR pretty much disappears after the first page of the SERP – with less than one per cent of Google searchers clicking on something from the second page onwards (Figure 2.5).

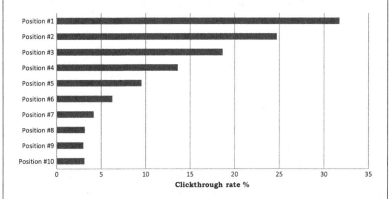

Figure 2.5 The clickthrough rate of SERP listing positions (Dean, 2019).

Furthermore, SERP listings impact sales. Profitero (2019) looked at the *sales lift* generated by appearing higher in the list. The research found that a product entering page one at the bottom of the SERP could expect to see sales increase by 84 per cent, in the middle 100 per cent and in top spot 152 per cent.

Off-site optimization

Although other elements exist – such as the age of a website – the key aspect to the SE's algorithm is the links that go into it from other sites. The philosophy behind the importance of these *inbound links* is that the search engines use them to judge a website – in essence, a site with lots of links going into it *must* carry some legitimacy with those sites that include the links and so the site's search engine validity rises also.

The more links to the site, the more valuable it is assumed to be, and so the higher the rating. Furthermore, the quality of the sites linking into a website is rated by the search engines, with so-called *authority* sites (e.g. the BBC) earning more points on the algorithm jigsaw. Opinions differ, but some practitioners argue that this is the element of the algorithm that scores most points – it's the four corners of the jigsaw. Although SEO staff can actively seek out inbound links, an effective and efficient integrated marketing strategy will *naturally* result in links going into the organization's site. For practitioners, this *natural* phenomenon is recognized as being SEO at its best as it goes closest to meeting the expectations of the search engines – that the website will best provide a solution or meet the needs of searchers. That such an approach is *strategic* rather than *tactical* also appeals to the search engines as the site's value is built over a long period of time, so endorsing its validity.

Third-party SERP ranking

This concept considers how the brand, product or organization might appear high in the SERP listings, but not on its own website; that is, on a website owned and/or published by a third party. There are three main ways in which this can be achieved, a listing (1) in a directory, (2) on a third-party website or (3) on a social media platform.

Directories

Online directories are direct descendants of *offline* directories, and in many cases the online incarnation is produced by the same organization that traditionally produced hard-copy versions – Yell and Yellow Pages, for example. Industry or trade bodies also list their members as part of their online presence, a local Chambers of Commerce cataloguing all businesses in its area or a council's tourist information department might have a directory of accommodation listed by type and location. Such is their nature that they *organically* suit many elements of search engines' algorithms and so feature high on many SERPs, particularly for *local* searches. It is the norm that *directories* include a link to the websites of listed organizations, so when searchers follow the SERP link to the directory website, they can then click on the link to that site – plus the site gets the advantage of an in-bound link.

Third-party websites

Although some of these present themselves as *directories* they are not the same as the traditional telephone-book type version. These are websites that, as a business model, seek to promote other businesses, normally in specific markets or industries. Part of that promotion – sometimes almost accidentally – is that the paying businesses appear high on the SERPs as a feature of the third party's web content. It is the retail, tourism and hospitality industries that have gained most from this form of listing. Obvious examples would include:

- The retailer – most likely a small or niche business – that stands next-to-no chance of getting products onto a SERP could sell them via eBay or Amazon.
- The hotel – likely to be an individual trader or part of a small chain – that uses a price comparison site to fill its rooms. As with the retailer example, getting its own site on the first page of the SERP is nigh-on impossible – but (for example) Booking.com's listing for a hotel that meets the search criteria will be there.
- The restaurant – though its website might get picked up on a local search in an area with few competitors, big-city eateries depend on other listings to put them in the SERPs. Most common would be Tripadvisor but all tourist towns and cities are covered by restaurant directories that take payment for inclusion.

Social media platforms

This would be more likely a *consequence* of a successful social media presence than SEO being the reason for developing the likes of a Facebook, Twitter or LinkedIn presence. For a first page SERP listing the social media site must be active – so setting up a *dormant* site for SEO purposes would be a waste of time.

Third party listings on a SERP

Publishing books for SEO listings is a little extreme – but it is an example of third-party listings on a SERP. Below is shown the first results page for a Google search on the author's name. Note how his own site comes in at the top, but the SERP is dominated by the author – albeit on other organizations' websites. In this case, they include: Twitter, Amazon, Google books, LinkedIn and his employer at the time of writing (Figure 2.6).

Figure 2.6 The Google SERP after a search by the author on his own
name. Note that this SERP will have been influenced by the
author's search history and previous online activities.

Further reading

For additional content and links to articles and stories that supplement this
chapter, go to its web page on www.AlanCharlesworth.com/AEDM.

References

@Alexa (2020) *How Do the Top Websites Drive Traffic?* @Alexa. Available at: https://try.alexa.com/resources/website-traffic-sources.

Anderson, C. (2006) *The Long Tail.* Hyperion Books. New York.

BrightEdge Technologies (2019) *Organic Search Improves Ability to Map to Consumer Intent.* Available at: https://videos.brightedge.com/research-report/BrightEdge_ChannelReport2019_FINAL.pdf.

Broder, A. (2002) *A Taxonomy of Web Search.* ACM Sigir Forum. Volume 36, Issue 2, pp. 3–10.

Dean, B. (2019) *Here's What We Learned about Organic Click through Rate.* Backlinko LLC. Available at: https://backlinko.com/google-ctr-stats.

Fishkin, R. (2019) *How Much of Google's Search Traffic Is Left for Anyone but Themselves?* SparkToro. Available at: https://sparktoro.com/blog/how-much-of-googles-search-traffic-is-left-for-anyone-but-themselves.

Profitero (2019) *Profitero Ecommerce Acceleration Playbook.* Available at: http://insights.profitero.com/rs/476-BCC-343/images/ECom-Acceleration-Playbook.pdf.

Salesforce (2018) *Shopper-First Retailing.* Available at: http://www.publicisgroupe.net/shopper-first.

Schwartz, E. (2018) *Search Engines Still Dominate over Social Media, Even for Millennials.* Search Engine Land. Available at: https://searchengineland.com/search-engines-still-dominate-over-social-media-even-for-millennials-308135.

3 Website development

Essential summary

This chapter covers those matters related to effective website development that are generic to all types of commercial web presence – be that website, social media platform or third-party sites such as e-marketplaces. Issues that are specific to retail and B2B sites are covered in the next two chapters – but all build on the fundamentals covered in this chapter. For the majority of organizations' digital marketing – be it strategic or operational – the website is the hub of online activity. Concentrating on management, presentation, usability and navigation, this chapter considers best practice in the development of the organization's web presence so that customer needs are met and organizational objectives achieved.

Website management and development

Whether the website is a couple of pages acting as a lead-generator for an offline SME or a pure-play retail site with thousands of pages, an element of *management* is required if they are to effectively meet the organization's objectives for that site. The range of issues to be addressed emphasize that the web manager must hold a position of some authority within the organization – or face the problem of being over-ruled by more officious managers or department heads. The range of skills required in developing and maintaining an effective website are varied, though not *all* are required for *every* site. These skills include such a diverse range of occupations such as programmers, graphic designers, usability experts, content writers, copywriters, search engine optimization specialists, sales staff, merchandisers and marketers. And this doesn't include specialists in the likes of metrics and analytics, conversion rate optimization, on-site security, checkout facilities, imaging, video, AR, VR ... indeed, the list constantly increases as new practices and technologies are introduced to the online digital world.

Do marketers need to know coding?

As with other technologies that marketers can make use of such as TV and radio, marketers do not need to know Internet technology actually works – only how to use it effectively. That said, a basic understanding of coding's fundamentals will help the digital marketer function effectively. However, many websites are now developed using WYSIWYG-type facilities offered by providers such as WordPress and so being aware of the intricacies of such services is perhaps more relevant than coding.

Ethos and philosophy

An important consideration – and one that is too often ignored by organizations (and writers) – is the role that the ethos and philosophy of the organization will play in the management and development of its web presence. Gerry McGovern has done so much work with web development teams that his views on this subject are ignored at the organization's own risk. Back in 2008 he made the point that:

> It is impossible to create a website with excellent service if there is not a culture of service within the web team that manages the websitecmany web teams are unfortunately filled with people who have little interest in serving. In fact, many web teams don't even accept that their primary job is to serve customers.

Sadly, all these years later, too often McGovern's assertions are still valid and it is no coincidence that some – if not all – of the most successful websites take this attitude on board.

Usability

Advertiser Alvin Hampel famously made the point that if an ad is clever but sells no products it has failed as an advert. To paraphrase him: if a commercial website is clever but does not meet the needs of its visitors then it has failed as a website. The key to this is the website's usability. Website usability has its origins in the sciences of graphical user interface (GUI, pronounced gooey) and human computer interface (HCI), though these terms are rarely used, being replaced by UX standing for *user experience* – which is all about making a website user friendly. In achieving the site's objectives its usability is – arguably – the most important element of website design. Usability *guru* Jacob Nielsen – whose background is in HCI – speaking on the importance of usability, says:

> If a website is difficult to use, people leave. If the homepage fails to clearly state what a company offers and what users can do on the site, people leave. If users get lost on a website, they leave. If a website's information is hard to read or doesn't answer users' key questions, they leave.

The basics

This section considers the key basic elements of presenting information on a website – but offers *guides*, not *rules*. The objectives of the site might dictate how the guides are interpreted, but they are ignored at the publisher's peril.

Site architecture

Before work starts on any website's development it is essential to plot its layout – the site architecture presented in hierarchical terms. This might be the first role for the website's manager, who should enlist the views of all interested parties. If the development is being out-sourced, the organization should have sketched out the architecture before the work is passed to the developers – the web manager will have a much better idea of the site's requirements than them. Figure 3.1 shows an

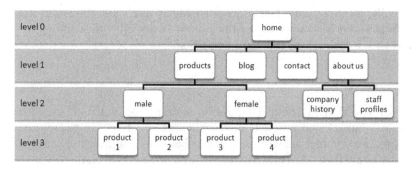

Figure 3.1 An example of a simple website architecture.

example of the structure of a basic website. Essentially, for any site, *level 1* is the navigation bar of the home page.

Content development

A website's content can be divided into two distinct elements: (1) textual, and (2) images and other features.

The development of textual content

In the development of website content there are four key issues that need to be addressed. In chronological order, they are:

- The solution to what need is being sought when a member of the target market chooses to visit the website?
- What information does the target market expect to be given to meet that need?
- How does the target market expect that information to be presented?
- How is this information best developed – and by whom?

The development of images and other features

After text, the next most common type of content is images. Although pictures are often included on a web page for purely aesthetic purposes, for other sites they are an essential element of helping to meet the customers' needs – an obvious example being product pictures. However – as with the textual content – professional input is best sought, particularly as the photos will need to be best captured with digital online reproduction in mind. The increased availability of broadband and their common use on social media has made videos not just a staple for some sites – but a requirement where moving images help sell a product. Like all content, however, it should be used only if it helps meet the objectives of the site, and so the user must perceive it as being useful – or they will never click on the play button.

Chat-bots (short for chat robots) are computer programs that simulate human conversation – chat – through the use of machine learning and artificial intelligence. They can be used for interaction with customers who might ask questions verbally or typed. However, despite significant hype, they are yet to be universally accepted by users.

The global web presence

When businesses are considering moving into new countries the primary strategic decision is *standardized* or *localized?* This means the organization must decide on whether the marketing mix it uses domestically will be successful globally, or will the mix need to be adapted to suit the various local markets. For the digital marketer there is a similar decision to be made with regard to the web presence for each country, except that rather than being two options there is a third option that falls between the two. The *standardized* approach is to have only one website of a domestic organization that caters for global audience – normally in English, though verbatim translation of some or all pages into other languages may be included. The localized approach is to develop different websites for each country in which the firm aims to trade. Using the domain names of the local countries, the content and presentation of these sites is adapted to address local culture and issues – though there may be some translation from the domestic site. The approach that falls between the two is the most popular option for those firms that are – or want to become – worldwide brands. Common amongst American brands, this is where the global organization develops local websites for each country in which they have a physical presence, but in this case each web presence would have a standardized brand image and the usage of common logos in uniform colours and layouts – but with content being localized where applicable.

Further reading

For additional content and links to articles and stories that supplement this chapter, go to its web page on www.AlanCharlesworth.com/AEDM.

Reference

McGovern, G. (2008) *How to Create Clear Web Navigation Menus.* Giraffe Forum. Available at: http://giraffeforum.com/wordpress/2009/11/15/how-to-create-clear-web-navigation-menus.

4 The retail website

Essential summary

Building on the basics of web presence development, this chapter concentrates on selling goods to the end user on a website. Although commonly referred to as e-commerce, it is – effectively – online retailing. Retailers that sell on websites can be divided into two main categories: pure-play, where the organization trades only online – and multi-channel, where the firm sells goods both off- and online. Key elements of the effective e-commerce site such as the checkout process are addressed as is the use of third-party shopping sites. The chapter ends with the last element of online retail – fulfilment.

The retail website

As well as recognizing that there are elements of website design that apply specifically to websites on which purchases can be made, the e-commerce developer must never undervalue the site as a retail outlet. Although online purchase facilities might be offered, consideration must also be afforded to the customer who might be on the site as *part* of their buying process, with a decision to buy being made either off- or online and the actual purchase made in the other medium. Similarly, few customers will make a purchase on their first visit to an e-commerce site – or even come to a purchase decision. At a time when online retail was in its infancy, Moe and Fader (2001) identified four types of online shopping visits that the customer might make – they are still valid:

1 Direct-purchase visits.
2 Search and deliberation visits.
3 Knowledge-building visits.
4 Hedonic-browsing visits.

Offline, it is easy for the experienced salesperson to identify these groups while they are in the shop – online the website can make no immediate recognition and so must cater for all of them.

Elements of the effective e-commerce site

Facilities found on effective e-commerce sites that do not appear on other types of website might include:

* In-site search facility. For the retail site that lists a wide range of products this is essential, particularly for the *direct purchase* shoppers.
* Cross- and up-selling. Also known as associated selling, this practice is well established in offline retail – and technology can be used to *digitalise* it.
* Calls to action. A retail website must not lose focus of its purpose – to sell things – and so the visitor must be constantly prompted to make a purchase.
* Contact options. Important for a number of reasons, not least the issue of online credibility, from a sales perspective this is essential.
* A product comparison facility. For retail sites that offer similar products from different manufacturers, this will help customers decide which product meets their needs the best or which is the best value for money.

The checkout process

If the shopper is to become a customer, there is no more important element of the online shop than the checkout facility – without which all the effort, cost and resources applied to the online shop's design are wasted. Important considerations for any checkout facility include that:

* For customers' peace of mind and the site's credibility, the checkout must be hosted on a secure server (the URL of the page will begin with https).

- It must be easy to use – although the entire site should have good usability, it is *essential* for the checkout process.
- It is constantly available – users must be able to get in and out of the checkout process as often as they wish.
- It is easy to change the basket (cart) at any time – add, delete or alter product attributes such as size.
- The basket's running total should be clearly shown on every page of the site.
- Shipping costs should be included in the basket's total – not added on when the customer is near the end of the checkout process.
- Options for delivery should be offered.
- Multiple methods of payment are available, including various debit/credit cards and online payment methods such a PayPal.
- Baskets with products can be saved for a return visit.

Abandoned baskets

Like the trolley full of shopping that is left at the offline checkout, any online basket that is filled but not purchased is a concern for the retailer. Reasons for this are manifold, from customer choice (customers *shopping* on a mobile device, but completing the purchase on a PC is still common or perhaps they want to double check a size) through bad checkout design (the shopper cannot or does not know how to use the facility and the instructions badly worded) to technology failures (an element of the checkout does not work on every browser or type of device).

Multi-channel retailing

Less than a generation ago, consumers were required to visit a retail outlet, consider the options available there and make a purchase. Shoppers can now use the Internet to research products and suppliers, and then have the choice of purchasing offline or online as well as having the product delivered or collecting it from a local store.

The latter has become known as *click-and-collect* (or sometimes the *trendier* BOPIS – buy online, pick-up in store) and the concept is now the cornerstone of multi-channel retailing. Although shoppers use the method to save shipping expenses or for convenience, for *some* buyers this is now *the* way of shopping. In other words, click-and-collect is shopping, and any retailer who is not participating takes the chance of not being considered by some customers to be a *proper* retailer. For the retailer it is not just the prospect of increasing sales via the web, but there is a very good chance that when customers visit the shop to collect their ordered goods they will make other purchases while they are there. Part of click-and-collect, but perhaps standing with a foot in *fulfilment* (covered later in this chapter) is the *ordering* online of products that are then ready to pick-up as the customer calls into the outlet. Rather pedantic word-play, but the idea is that if the customers *collect*, they enter the store as a shopper whereas *pick-up* implies a much swifter experience – think of it as the difference between entering a McDonald's to order a meal and getting it at a drive-through window. Indeed, fast food is an example of where the model is already in operation, Starbuck's for example where pre-ordering means not waiting for the barista to make your coffee. Recognizing the potential logistical problems with this (e.g. two serving points to ensure free-flow of pick-up customers) many exponents have opened pick-up only outlets for customers using the service.

Third-party shopping sites

The e-commerce seller has, essentially, two options in the type of website on which they can sell goods or services: a site they own and operate themselves or one owned and operated by a *third party*. Traditionally, the former is a retail outlet (shop) and the latter a market (from which the term *marketing* evolved) where the owner of land rents out space to sellers and then promotes the market to would-be buyers. Online, things get a little more complex – *confusing* even. Offline, each seller in the market takes payment from the customer for whatever they sell. Online, however, it is the norm for the *e-marketplace* owner/operator to facilitate payment for all goods purchased on the site (rather like offline *concessions*). This is both convenient for buyers, resource saving for smaller sellers (they do not have to set up payment facilities on their own website) and effective in increasing sales as customers can *shop* the entire site, fill a basket/cart from a variety of sellers and make only one payment. It is also profitable for the e-marketplace owner as they can charge rent for listing the products on their site (i.e. in their *market*) *and* take a percentage of any sales made. For the seller, the fees *can* be worthwhile as the e-marketplace attracts customers through its own promotion (e.g. on- and offline advertising, SEO and brand building).

More commonly used for the sale of services rather than physical products, price comparison sites (sometimes called *comparison shopping engines* or *shopping search engines*) provide a search facility which, as a business model, elicits fees from the sellers of products that are listed on the comparison pages produced as a result of a potential customer's search on the site. Significantly, unlike the e-marketplace, *most* comparison sites redirect the consumer to the seller's website to make the purchase and payment – the insurance industry, for example, has been changed by this model. If the way we purchase insurance has been changed by comparison sites, it is the travel industry that has been a primary exponent of the concept – to such an extent that using such a comparison site to book accommodation is now the *norm*. In this example, however, there is a further twist in that hotel comparison sites (sometimes called online travel agencies – OTAs) provide each hotel with a web page and booking facility that is so efficient that it makes sense for many smaller hotels to use such third-party facilities rather than running their own.

Adding to the misunderstanding of what third-party sites *actually* are, the listing of available products with links to the sellers is more akin to advertising than it is to retailing. Similarly, the term *search engine* in this context is a misnomer as the comparison sites search only a directory of products whose sellers have agreed for them to be listed and not every product that is available. Even the term *e-marketplace* is rarely used by the shopping public – the sites of the main players being known simply by their brand name, not description. The business models of the major brands – Amazon, eBay, Alibaba, JD and Taobao – serve only to muddy the waters still further. Amazon retails products it has purchased from suppliers, has its *Amazon Marketplace* for sellers to use the site as a third party, sells its own brand products *and* provides a delivery service for products. Needless to say, few buyers fully appreciate the complexity of Amazon's business model – simply putting products into the basket and clicking on *buy now*. Although the original concept was for the general public to sell off – by auction – unwanted items in a kind of online boot-sale, eBay is now more commonly used by small and micro retailers who develop their own eBay store as a method of reaching a market that prior to the Internet was simply not accessible. Furthermore, many shun the auction model, simply listing goods at a fixed price. These sellers make much of the eBay site a *facilitator* of – or platform for – B2C retail transactions rather than the C2C auction site that it was originally. Sitting a grey zone somewhere between retail, advertising and social media is the use of platforms such as Instagram to list products and facilitate sales through its *Instagram Checkout*. To date, the popularly of this is limited to a small number of product areas (clothing is an example). Legally, any such *listing* is an advert, and they are distributed through ad networks (see Chapter 6) but it is a type of advert that can be clicked on to make a purchase without being taken to the seller's website, so putting it in the category of third-party shopping site.

Fulfilment

Too often relegated to the back-burner through lack of digital *sexiness*, fulfilment can be split into two key elements; delivery and returns – that is, putting the product into the hands of the buyer and facilitating its return if the buyer rejects it for whatever reason.

Delivery

Despite it being a less than glamorous aspect of digital marketing, making sure that the customer receives the product they have ordered is just as important as any other aspect of online sales. Influenced by the ubiquitous Amazon, online buyers' expectations have become such that they expect purchases to have next day delivery and for that delivery to be free. Indeed, a good delivery process could be the main reason for brand loyalty – trumping even price if the product is not too price sensitive. Key to the issue is the so-called 'last mile' to the customer's delivery address – normally, their home. Over the years that online retail has existed, numerous initiatives have been tried to address the issue of unattended and deferred home deliveries. Technology has helped, online tracking enabling customers to follow the path of a delivery as it makes its way to the delivery point, for example. However, such initiatives serve only to make the acceptance of a delivery more convenient – but for large, valuable or packages that require a signature of delivery confirmation a human being's presence at the address is necessary. Although many schemes exist, including the likes of: redelivery services (the customer directs goods to a depot, from where they collect it); pickup – and return – points at convenience stores; collection points at conveniently located self-storage lockers; strategic alliances where online sellers have goods collected at high street retailers – but to date none has met with universal customer acceptance. Meanwhile, cities such as New York are suffering from piles of parcels blocking side-walks (pavements) outside multi-unit apartment buildings that have provision for accepting and assigning letters to their addressees, but not parcels that can be anything from a cigar box to an item of furniture. For all the technological developments of the 21st Century, having a friendly neighbour is still the answer for many an online customer.

Returns

Also known as *reverse* logistics, the online seller must give consideration to customers who – for whatever reason – want to return the goods. Those reasons can be genuine – the goods being faulty or the wrong size, for example – but other more nefarious motives exist. Using purchases once (clothes being an obvious example) and returning them or sending stolen goods for a refund are a couple of examples. Another reflects a sign of the times: with the rise of social media, Instagram in particular, the practice of buying clothes purely to wear them in a *selfie* before returning them is, apparently, commonplace. Nor is returns an insignificant problem. According to David Sobie, co-founder and CEO of Happy Returns (in an interview with CNBC) 'Shoppers return 5 to 10 per cent of what they purchase in store but 15 to 40 per cent of what they buy online'. As catalogue retailers discovered over the past 100 years or so, the logistical costs of receiving and preparing goods for resale are so substantial that they found it cheaper to simply destroy returns or sell them on as *job lots* to contracted shops who sold them as 'seconds'. A final consideration for the online retailer is that a customer-centric returns policy – like free delivery – can be perceived by shoppers as being indicative of the organization's brand value something else that Amazon have led on.

Further reading

For additional content and links to articles and stories that supplement this chapter, go to its web page on www.AlanCharlesworth.com/AEDM.

Reference

Moe, W.W. and Fader, P.S. MIT (2001) *Which Visits Lead to Purchases? Dynamic Conversion Behavior at E-Commerce Sites.* Sloan Management Review. Volume 42, Issue 2, pp. 8–9.

5   The B2B website

Essential summary

Again building on the fundamentals of web presence development, this chapter concentrates on the use of websites by businesses that are selling to other organizations rather than to the end user and where the objective of the site is likely to be lead generation rather than branding or direct sales. The B2B buying process is examined and the role of the decision making unit (DMU) addressed as well as the different types of B2B purchase. That business purchases can be made online is covered in the B2B e-commerce website and this chapter ends by considering the role of B2B e-marketplaces.

The B2B website

Although all aspects of effective web presence development covered in Chapter 3 apply equally to the B2B digital marketer, the buyer behaviour in a B2B environment differs from that of consumers – and this needs to be taken into consideration when developing online content. A further complication for the B2B seller is that purchase decisions are rarely made by one person, the norm being that the potential buyer has a decision making unit.

The decision making unit (DMU)

Also known as the *buying centre*, the DMU is a group of people within the organization that has responsibility for making buying decisions. Although the actual formation will be unique to each organization depending on its business and market, a DMU would normally consist of some or all of:

- Gatekeepers who control the flow of information in and out of the organization.
- Initiators who start the decision making process by requesting a purchase.
- Deciders who make the actual purchase decision.
- Buyers who select suppliers and manage the buying process.
- Influencers who evaluate and recommend suppliers.
- Users who actually *use* the product or service.

Naturally, some products require less input from the DMU (e.g. sweeping brushes) than others (e.g. components for a jet engine). Depending on the organization and product, some or all of these may use the seller's website in the early stages of the buying process, and so the website must be developed with this in mind. Furthermore, the website must also meet the needs of different types of B2B purchase, of which it is generally recognized that there are three:

- The *New task* is where the organization is seeking to buy a product for the first time.
- The *modified rebuy* is where the organization seeks to reorder a previously purchased product but with some modification to agreed product specifications, prices, delivery schedule, lead time or other aspects of the order.
- The *straight rebuy* is where the organization seeks to reorder a previously purchased product without any modifications.

Lead generation

A long-standing marketing model, *lead generation* is the development of an initial contact between vendors and potential customers. B2B marketing is dependent on sellers seeking out *genuine* potential customers – sales leads – for the products or services they have on offer. It is important to note that a *lead* is not a *sale*, only the opportunity to deliver a pitch that might lead to a sale. The better the lead, the greater the chance of converting prospect to sale. Therefore, the majority of B2B websites have an objective of lead *generation* rather than online sales. The website must generate enough interest in whatever the organization has to offer for the user to make contact with the company. Once the initial contact is made the *generation* element of the process is over and representatives of the organization must use their sales skills to *convert* the lead to a sale.

The B2B buying process

The B2B buying process is far more complex than in B2C, and the website's content must meet the requirements of all its various elements, the following are the steps in the process:

1 Problem recognition – buyers may use the web to keep up to date with news in their sector, so online press releases for new developments or products should be distributed to sites that might be visited by industry workers. The organization's own website should include content on new products, new applications or any other advances that are important in the industry or marketplace. The use of social media can be effective at this stage with blogs or social network sites having a role to play (this might be an element of *content marketing* introduced in Chapter 1).
2 Specification development – the website must address any issues that might be specific to the buyer – although it should be inherent in any product description.
3 Search for products (if off-the-shelf) or search for supplier (if bespoke). Not only are there search engine optimization issues to consider, but the information that the buyers seek must be made easily available on the site – and in a format that they would find most useful.
4 Evaluate products and suppliers – based on their perception of the organization and its offerings gleaned from the website, a potential buyer may or may not make initial contact that might ultimately lead to a contract for multiple hundreds, thousands or millions of units.
5 Make purchase – although this might be an online order, for the majority of B2B purchases this would be something conducted in person. However, for this *offline* buying model, this stage *online* might be considered to be the contact with the organization – the lead generation of the website has worked and so its objective (sale) has been achieved.

6   After sales service – as with other web presences, this can be a specific objective of the organization's online presence, be that website or social media platform. In the B2B environment, this could well be part of any contractual agreement made with regard to the product – installation instructions or application updates, for example.

Further issues that the B2B marketer must consider in the development of the website include that:

*   A B2B buyer is often starting at square one with no knowledge of the market – therefore brand affinity does not play any part and so the website and its content must present the reader with a professional brand that inspires trust.
*   In B2B purchases risk avoidance is a significant issue – ordering bespoke products that are not suitable for your application in a B2B environment could spell bankruptcy for the company. Website copy should reflect this concern.
*   Relevant information must be presented appropriately, with the language used appealing to the various members of the DMU. For example, in a B2C environment jargon, acronyms and abbreviations should be avoided – in B2B trading a lack of these might give the impression that you are not a serious player in that industry.
*   That any marketing message must match up with potential customers' expectations, requirements and needs should go without saying, but for the website the range of readers makes this more problematic. For example, the *economic* buyer will be concentrating on price, discounts, rebates, while the *user* buyer will care less for cost and concentrate on whether or not the product will serve the purpose for which it is being purchased. Any web content that does not address the issues of *all* members of a DMU may find a *neglected* group rejecting the organization's offering and looking elsewhere.

B2B vs B2C websites: key user experience differences

User experience (UX) is equally important on B2B websites as it is in B2C. The Nielsen Norman Group – experts in the subject of UX – suggests that B2B buyers have needs that are very different from those of B2C *consumers*. They identify five significant differences in the user experience requirements for B2B and B2C sites.

Difference 1: content must support long purchase decisions.
Difference 2: integration, compatibility and regulatory information needs to be clear.
Difference 3: content should speak to both *choosers* and *users*.
Difference 4: complex pricing requires realistic scenarios.
Difference 5: speak to different customer segments and scales of businesses without alienating audiences.

The B2B e-commerce website

For some B2B purchases it is possible to offer products for sale on an e-commerce website where the customer can select and order goods in much the same way as on a *retail* website. Fitting into *straight rebuy* category described earlier, such products are likely to be retail in nature – stationery, cleaning materials and electrical goods such as kettles and coffee makers, for example – essentially, consumer goods rather than commercial products. They are also likely to be of relatively low value but not budget priced – the site being used more for convenience than cost saving. Another example is the website that is B2C for domestic customers and B2B for commercial sales – registered businesses getting a lower *trade* price at the checkout; plumbing goods supplier Screwfix is an example. Like B2C sales, purchases can be collected, but in a B2B environment *delivery included* is a standard term of reference. As the site is essentially a shop, all the good practices of an online retailer – as described in the previous chapter – apply uniformly to the B2B e-commerce site. Users will not forgive poor design just because it is a commercial rather than retail site – they use Amazon and the like for personal purchases and expect similar service.

B2B e-marketplaces

Although the term is used in the B2C environment, *e-marketplaces* are more commonly associated with B2B trading. Like their retail equivalents, B2B e-marketplaces have existed *offline* for many years.

Often industry-specific, B2B e-marketplaces are far less well known by the general public (they do not make for *sexy* news stories) and only people with an interest in those industries will have cause to have even heard of them. Although some e-marketplaces are open to any and all members of an industry, many are restricted to membership of a restricted community – be they buyers or sellers.

As with the traditional version, B2B e-marketplaces have two interested parties, buyers and sellers. *Buyers* seek visible sellers better prices, a more efficient purchasing process, knowledgeable sellers and controlled spending. *Sellers* seek new markets and new customers. With the exception of those B2C e-marketplaces that seek to bring customers together to make *group* purchases (e.g. Groupon and Living Social) members of B2B marketplaces – in a rather civilised fashion – frequently partner up with competitors in both the supply and buying sides of the market, working together to either best meet the needs of customers or get the best deals available from sellers. An integral element of the content and purpose of many B2B e-marketplaces are auctions and tendering facilities. At *forward* auctions, the seller places goods (usually surplus or used) for sale and invites bids. With online *reverse* auctions – also known as *procurement* auctions – the role of the buyer and seller are reversed, with the buyer announcing what they wish to purchase and then inviting bids to satisfy those wants. With its origins in fair and equitable trading – and the elimination of bribery and corruption – *tendering* has been common practice in the public sector for many years. Fundamentally, the process is this: (1) the buyer makes known their requirements; (2) potential bidders make known their interest and submit details of their organization to evaluated by the buyer; (3) if they meet the required standards, the company is accepted to submit a tender; (4) all interested parties submit a sealed bid by a pre-determined deadline; (5) the buyer reviews all of the bids – although price will be the dominant characteristic of any decision, it is possible for a higher bid to incorporate better specifications; (6) all entrants are informed of the successful bid, with the winner being awarded a contract for the work. Prior to the Internet, and like auctions, this process was unwieldy, complicated and time-consuming. However, online technology has alleviated much of the bureaucracy and made tendering far more accessible – particularly to smaller businesses which can proceed independently of form partnerships within e-marketplaces.

Further reading

For additional content and links to articles and stories that supplement this chapter, go to its web page on www.AlanCharlesworth.com/AEDM.

6   Advertising online

Essential summary

This chapter starts with an introduction to why all types of on-line advertising are covered in this chapter and explains what automated, programmatic, network and display advertising is before briefly covering types of ad delivery. The four main types of online ads are then addressed. Search advertising is the ads that appear on SERPs. Display network advertising is the model that puts ads onto a variety of websites including social media platforms. The section on programmatic advertising explains how real-time programmatic advertising delivers ads. The final type of advertising covered is native – the non-advert ad. The limitations of online advertising are then dealt with, including such issues as how well digital advert works, whether users like ads, ad fraud and ads appearing on inappropriate host websites.

Introduction

Before getting into the specifics of online advertising, it's worth ap-preciation three key issues; why all digital advertising should be one subject, what the types of ads are called and how ads are delivered to web pages.

Why all *online advertising* is *advertising*

This chapter considers online advertising – no matter where it is hosted. It has become common for advertising on certain platforms to be identified as *marketing* on those platforms. The obvious villains of this advertising piece are: advertising on search engines, advertising on social media and advertising on mobile devices which are too frequently combined with other disciplines to form search engine marketing (SEO *and* advertising on SERPs), social media marketing (social media engagement and *advertising* on social media) and mobile marketing (all aspects of digital marketing *including* advertising on mobile devices).

The argument in favour of the *advertising is advertising* approach includes that:

* The development of effective adverts requires a specific skill set which is not necessarily available in an SEO or social media environment.
* There are other recognized types of online advertising including network/display, programmatic, retargeting and Amazon – which means an organization could have several advertising individuals, teams or agencies all working in, or for, different digital marketing departments.
* Advertising campaigns should be coordinated across platforms – an essential element of any strategic initiative. Such coordination can also include harmonization with offline advert campaigns.

Automated, programmatic, network or display?

Seemingly used at random when referring to aspects of online advertising it's reasonable to assert that no-one can *really* clarify these terms. The problems arise, mainly, from the terminology used – and the misunderstanding and misinterpretation of them. The author has taken a considered stance on the use of the terms which suit the purposes of this particular book – but which may or may not be agreed by others.

For more on this subject, see *Further Reading* at the end of this chapter.

Ad delivery

There are four fundamental ways in which an ad can be delivered to a web page. They are:

1   Keyword bidding – the ad appears on the page in response to keywords associated with the user in one of two ways:
    * Direct; a query on a search engine.
    * Indirect; matched to keywords in web page content.

2   Display network advertising – banner ads are delivered on web-
    sites that have agreed to be part of the network that is distributing
    the ads on behalf of the advertisers.
3   Direct *(contact)* ads – advertisers and publishers deal with each
    other directly to arrange details of ads to be included on a website.
4   Native advertising – the appearance of these ads is such that they
    are not *obviously* an advert – their appearance blending in with
    other content.

Search advertising

It is important to appreciate that *advertising* on search engine results
pages (SERPs) is not the same as being featured in their *organic* results
(covered in Chapter 2), this chapter examines listing on SERPs that are
paid for – hence it is sometimes referred to as *paid search*. The basic
premise of search engine advertising is based on the search concept of
matching the searchers' keywords with links to pages that will satisfy
the objectives of those searchers. In search engine optimization, the
chosen words are placed on the web pages (see Chapter 2). With SERP
advertising, the keywords are *purchased* by the advertiser (hence *paid
search*), with the ad that appears highest on the SERP's ads listings being the one that has made the *best* bid made for it (although price plays
a significant part in the bid, other criteria have an influence). Having
won the bidding process, the advertiser has – effectively – won permission to have their ad featured on the relevant SERP. The amount
of the bid is the fee payable to the search engine every time someone
clicks on the ad (the pay-per-click – PPC – model). Naturally, as in
all business environments, keyword bidding is influenced by the level
of competition in any given marketplace. So it is that some keywords
in competitive markets cost far more than industries where competition is lower. Note that less popular keywords within a market will
be cheaper – the so-called *long tail of keywords*. Whilst this section
concentrates on advertising on SERPs, it is the case that similar technology and systems are used by ad networks in placing ads on other
sites – indeed, the key players in ad networking are the main search engines. Therefore, although network advertising is covered in the next
section, this section helps in getting to grips with the basics of both
models. As search engine optimization is not an exact science, results
are far from certain. Therefore, the key advantage of buying ads on
SERPs is that whilst there is still no *certainty* that their ads will appear
on the page, at least the advertiser maintains a degree of control over
the situation. Other advantages to using paid search include:

- The text that searchers see can be determined by the advertiser – unlike the organic returns which present text taken (sometimes randomly) from the page.
- Although they may not click on the ad, search engine users may perceive that the organization or product at the top of the ads is the leader in its field with repeated exposure in the ads can helping in brand recognition.

Keyword bidding

The keywords chosen for ads can be the same as those used for search engine optimization (see Chapter 2) or different depending on whether the objective is to reinforce essential terms or spread keyword appeal across *organic* search and advertising. Although keyword bidding is the general term used for the exercise of *buying* keywords on a SERP, the actual practice includes more aspects than simply making a bid – otherwise the organization with the biggest budget would always top the list. As with the organic listings, the search engines' primary concern for ads is to satisfy searchers – allowing the biggest spenders to buy the top spot does not necessarily meet that criteria. In addition to the monetary value of the bid, the strength – what Google refers to as the *quality score* – of each keyword bid will be measured against the following:

- Clickthrough rate (CTR) history. Previous ads are used to assess how successful they have been in attracting clicks from searchers – those with a good track record will gain credit.
- Landing page quality. The search engine will look for relevance to the search keywords in headings and body copy as well as assessing the architecture and user experience of the destination site – including the landing page's download time.
- Ad Relevance. This measures how closely the keyword matches the message in your ads – the more specific, the better. Also considered is the keyword's relevance to the advertiser's business.

Google shopping ads

Search engine optimization is typically a long and precarious process, taking months to see any results – which may not be good. Shopping ads, on the other hand, can generate results – sales – immediately. Shopping ads are more than the normal SERP text ad, appearing above or alongside the text-based ads and organic listings and showing users a photo of the product, price, description, store name and more – and they use this data instead of keywords to determine how and where ads are shown in response to a user's search.

There are three types of Shopping ads:

- Product Shopping ads – created based on the product data.
- Showcase Shopping ads – groupings of related products.
- Local catalogue ads – use the product data for ads on the Google Display Network.

Each listed product has a unique product page, meaning every Shopping ad click takes the visitor to a specific product – so increasing potential sales. Similar shopping ads are available on Bing Ads and Yahoo Gemini.

Banner blindness

Research by Burke et al. back in 2005 suggested that around 86 per cent of us do not consciously notice ads on web pages – we simply tune them out. Is that figure of 86 higher or lower now?

Display network advertising

Although this chapter covers both display network advertising (commonly abbreviated to *display*) and programmatic advertising in different sections, it's worth noting that because display network advertising uses *programmatic* technologies, it is common for the term *programmatic advertising* to be used to describe it. As these sections show, they are not interchangeable descriptions. Although it dominates the industry – as with SEO – it is common to hear people refer to *Google advertising* as the generic term for all online advertising – Google display is not the only display ad network. As well as the other main search providers Yahoo and Bing, there are independent network providers, led by Conversant Media. However, it is another of the premier online brands – Amazon – that is one of the biggest ad networks after Google.

A brief description of display network advertising includes that:

- Ads are delivered on websites that are part of the network.
- Ads can be associated with web page content.
- Ads can be specific to groups of users based on clickstream data or behavioural or contextual actions.
- Ads can be personalized to the individual user.

Online segmentation of ad delivery is broken into three *core* types of targeting – though the last can be used in unison with either of the first two and each has its own sub-categories:

1   Contextual – the ads served are relevant (in context) to the content of the web page.
2   Behavioural – ads are delivered in response to the user's prior actions on the web.
3   Geographical – the use of IP recognition to identify where in the world the surfer is, with location-related ads then being served.

Advertising on social media

A variety of social media platforms are available to advertisers – with some being more effective in distinct markets or industries. However, by far the biggest social media site for advertising is Facebook. Indeed, the size and power of Facebook makes its display network advertising second overall only to Google.

- Facebook. The social media platform's network advertising follows the Google model – not only delivering ads on Facebook pages, but also throughout a wide network of apps and non-website media.
- Twitter. Purchased by auction or automated bidding, Twitter Ads, like Facebook (its owner) concentrate on internal promotion.
- Pinterest. The image-based platform uses visual *pins* rather than textual ads. It also has shopping ads, on which users can click to instigate a direct purchase.
- YouTube. Three video ad categories all of which are paid for on a CPM basis are available; *TrueView* skippable ads, non-skippable *Pre-roll* and *Mid-roll* ads and *Bumper* ads are non-skippable and appear at the end of videos.
- Instagram. As well as *standard* photo and video ads the platform also offers carousel, story and collection ads.

Programmatic advertising

Various sources suggest *programmatic* currently accounts for around half of all online advertising and its increased use is predicted to move that percentage up still further. Often *mistakenly* referred to as programmatic *marketing*, programmatic advertising describes the use of algorithm-driven software to replace humans in the purchase and delivery of adverts on a variety of online platforms with the opportunity to show an ad to a specific customer, in a specific context. That it automates the process was cause for it to be called *automated* advertising in its early days. The concept was originally developed to help publishers sell vacant advertising space (remnant inventory) on websites using programmatic *direct* (though also called programmatic *guaranteed* or programmatic *reserved* – which better describe the intent) where advertisers use automated software to buy guaranteed ad space impressions from specific publishers. Because ads can be delivered in real-time, and that ad spaces are allocated by bids, this practice is commonly referred to as *real-time bidding* (RTB). Note that because they are paid for in advance, direct ads download before real-time ads. However, the first ad to download and be seen by users is the header (the ad banner that goes across the top of a web page), there are now auctions for the page headers – this is known as *header bidding*.

How real-time programmatic advertising delivers ads

There are five basic stages to the process of real-time delivery of programmatic advertising:

1   The process starts with the publisher of a website – in order to generate income – constructing its pages so that they can host and deliver adverts in allocated spaces within each page.
2   The user clicks on a link to take them to an ad-configured web page.
3   As soon as the ad placements begin to download, the website's publisher – *automatically* – submits an ad impression for auction in an ad marketplace.
4   The ad marketplace performs an auction amongst advertisers who have an interest in displaying an ad to the specific user who has just clicked on to a link to the page . At this point the use of existing data, machine learning and AI may come into play in identifying specific customers who would respond best to the advert.
5   The advertiser with the highest bid wins the auction and their ad is displayed to the customer when the page loads. At this point, the advertiser has incurred a fee that is shared between the ad marketplace and the web page's publisher.

Note that because the bid is pre-programmed, from the user clicking on the link to the ad being displayed takes only milliseconds. It is also the case that the page may have multiple ad spaces and – on a busy site – many users arriving every second. Although it might be possible for marketers to engage in buying programmatic ads themselves via a demand side platform, an in-house team would need the significant knowledge, technology and resources to do this efficiently. Whilst some major global brands are bringing programmatic in-house, the majority will use agencies.

Re-targeting and re-marketing

A type of behavioural advertising, re-targeting is where a consumer has visited a website but not met the site's objective – a purchase, for example – is shown relevant ads for that site in their subsequent surfing around the web. From the advertiser's point of view, this is an excellent use of behavioural data taken from their website and an effective way of delivering ads to a well-defined target audience. However, this form of advertising is frequently voted the most disliked type of advertising on the Internet. Re-marketing ads, on the other hand, are ads that are triggered by the user exiting an e-commerce site leaving products in a basket without purchasing them. The idea is to remind the customers that the basket has been saved and the purchase can still be made. At one time the reminders included an incentive to purchase – but this soon ceased when savvy buyers realized that they could get discounted products if they *abandoned* a basket first.

Direct *(contact)* ads

Harking back to the early days of the web before any *automation* was available, this is where the advertiser contacts the website owner/publisher directly and the two parties agree on the details of ads being included on a website. Realistically, this happens at only the top and bottom ends of the online advertising scale. A major global brand (or its agency), for example, might deal direct with a major publisher for 'static' (i.e. not algorithm-driven) banner ads to appear on the website. The ads will be delivered at a fixed price over a fixed period of time and as they are, effectively, *part* of the site rather than a downloading extra they tend to download faster than programmatically delivered ads. At the other end of the scale, two opportunities are available:

- A local business might contact an appropriate local publisher – e.g. a gardener and neighbourhood blog.

• A seller in a niche industry might contact the publisher of website or blog covering that subject – crafts or hobbies would be an example. Note, however, that this kind of agreement might be better suited to *sponsorship* or even an *amateur* affiliate agreement.

Native advertising

Delivered by the main players in online advertising and several native-only networks such as Taboola and Outbrain, native ads appear *within* other content with the look, feel and function of the media format in which they appear. Payment is via PPC. Executed well, native ads can be effective and successful. Performed badly, users resent that marketers are attempting to fool the reader – or even treat them as fools – and the results are the opposite of those desired by the brand's marketers. To meet legal and industry regulations, each native ad must be identified as being such. This can be by them being labelled as: suggested post, recommended for you, promoted story, recommended or suggested videos, sponsored – but rarely the term *advert* – and sometimes merely a tiny image of a box with an arrow coming out of its top right hand corner. Although consumers generally recognize native ads as a form of advertising, they are far more likely to notice and react to them than any other type of online ad. A significant advantage of native advertising is that the ads are rarely subject to ad-blocking software. Primarily for this reason, *native* has grown in popularity in recent years. However, compared to the original concept of native advertising (text within content) these are rather like native *light*, with there being more effort to blend in with the web page's presentation than the content. For example, on portal sites which feature equal-sized *boxes* most of which contain news item from various media sources, but around one in six are ads *camouflaged* on the page within the range of news boxes.

Landing pages

Although the term is sometimes described as the page on which a surfer arrives at a website, in marketing terms, a landing page is the web page to which the user is taken when they click on the link in an advert. Although this subject is equally relevant in email marketing, it is included here to emphasize the importance of landing pages in online advertising. Despite the recognized value of using effective landing pages, too often online advertisers do not give them the attention they warrant – even though substantial resources might have been invested in the adverts that drive potential customer to those pages. With click-through rates being relatively low, to discard these hard-earned clicks makes no sense. The issue is that if an advert motivates a potential customer to click on its link, it is essential that any sales momentum generated by the advert is maintained, hopefully through to the *buy now* command. Any barrier – no matter how slight – might prompt the user to simply hit the *return* button. A landing page must be developed for each ad and it should respond to the message in the advert. Ads promoting a purchase must have a landing page that includes a *buy now* facility. Other ads might encourage the user to seek further information on the product or service and so the landing page must provide it in an appropriate manner and perhaps guide the user further into the website. As well as reasons of best practice in user experience, if the performance of individual ads or ad campaign is to be assessed, a separate URL (of each landing page) must be included in any analytics software being used so that they can be tracked correctly. As mentioned in the earlier section on Google's *Quality Score* for ad bids, the major search engines evaluate the landing pages that link from their SERP ads. This is mainly to prevent dubious advertisers from simply buying their way to the top of the (paid) listings. Essentially, a *good* landing page gives a better chance of topping the list than one the search engine feels is disingenuous.

Limitations of online advertising

As it matured as a marketing tool, online advertising attracted as many detractors as supporters. Here are some of the key issues raised by those who question its effectiveness.

Does it work?

Rather like traditional advertising, the effectiveness of online ads that have *branding* as their objective is difficult to assess – just because an ad is downloaded onto a web page does not guarantee the user has even seen it, let alone taken any notice of it or its message. PPC, on the other hand, has always boasted measurability as its advantage over most other forms of advertising – off- and online. CTRs are not, however, as high as the casual observer might expect. Research presented by Wordstream (2019) suggest the following are average CTRs for different platforms.

- Bing Search: 3.11%
- Facebook Messenger: 0.67%

- Facebook newsfeed: 1.46%
- Google display: 0.35%
- Google search: 1.91%
- Instagram newsfeed: 0.62%
- LinkedIn ads: 0.26%
- Twitter: 1.55%
- YouTube ads: 0.24%

Naturally, some of these platforms lend themselves more to branding objectives and so CTR is not necessarily a valid measurement of success – but less than two per cent on Google SERPs is disappointingly low. However, if thousands, or even millions of impressions are delivered, the small percentage represents a high number of potential customers.

Do users like ads?

The statistics in the previous section suggest that users are not overly keen on online ads, and there is worse news for the digital marketer. Apparently, according to research from Ofcom (2018), 42 per cent of users in the UK are not aware that listings at the top of the SERP may be ads – this means that some of the already low CTR is accidental. Research results published in recent years all suggest that users are not keen on adverts on the web – including that by Kantar (2019) which found that when respondents were asked about online advertising generally 23 liked it, 30 per cent disliked it and 47 per cent said it didn't bother them one way or the other. In the UK online ads are even less popular, with 55 per cent of respondents said they are completely apathetic towards advertising content.

Ad fraud

Although there is much spoken and written about a variety of ad frauds – including those attributed to such things as mobile, video, retargeting and cookies – there are only two basic forms of ad fraud: click fraud (PPC) and impression fraud (CPM).

Ad fraud – PPC

Click fraud has been around as long as PPC advertising – and the practice continues, though at what level is disputed by buyers and providers. Depending on which side you stand, click fraud is either not really a problem or it is a reason for not using PPC advertising. The search engines say that the amount of click fraud is negligible. However, some advertisers – and independent investigators – suggest that up to 60 per cent of clicks might well be fraudulent.

So what is click fraud? Basically, PPC works by having advertisers pay website publishers each time a visitor clicks on an ad. That no clicks equals no cost, and that each clickthrough is recorded, makes the model – theoretically – both cost-effective and easily measured. However, a dishonest publisher or agent handling a site's PPC ads, knowing that a payment was received for every click made on an ad on a website, might be tempted to inflate those clicks erroneously. The odd click here and there is not likely to be a significant problem for advertisers, but the nefarious publisher is going to use cheap labour overseas or a computer program to roam the site clicking on ads hundreds or thousands of times every day. This is affordable so long as the cost of each fraudulent click is less than how much is received for each click – that is, how much the advertiser is charged.

Massive ad spend lost to fraud

In a 2020 interview with Alan Hart early in 2020, Kevin Frisch, the former head of performance marketing and CRM at Uber told of how ad fraud 'ate up' nearly $120 million of Uber's $150 million online ad budget. He went on to say that; 'We turned off two thirds of our spend, we turned off 100 million of annual spend out of 150, and basically saw no change…'.

Ad fraud – CPM

The rise of programmatic advertising has been matched by the development of *impression* fraud. Although it can be used for click fraud, the following swindles are normally reserved for impression fraud.

1   Software is used to invent thousands of phoney web users, each with their own profile, who visit websites or social media platforms. Each profile triggers the automated ads that respond to the false profiles.
2   To really make some money, however, the *serious* swindler sets up around a quarter of a million counterfeit web pages and then acquires around half a million IP addresses and configures them so that they appeared to be *people* located all over the United

States. Operating as a sham intermediary (network) companies pay to run their expensive video ads on the phoney websites to be *watched* by the *phoney* visitors. Naturally, all of this is done by computer software. Far from being the fantastic plot of a heist movie, this is a brief description of a fraud perpetrated by Russian cybercriminals using software dubbed the *Methbot* at the end of 2016. In the time it took to be spotted, the fraud – reportedly – siphoned off more than $180 million from the online advertisers. That's quite a negative return on investment. And this is a scam that *was* discovered.

Inappropriate host websites

Although the phenomenon existed before, and continues today, 2017 saw the peak in having ads appear on unsuitable sites. That year saw hundreds of brands including Mercedes-Benz, Waitrose, Marie Curie, Honda and Thomson Reuters having ads for their products appearing on *hate* websites and YouTube videos created by supporters of terrorist groups. If that wasn't embarrassing enough, such is the nature of online advertising, not only did the network publishers (e.g. Google) earn income from the ads – but more seriously – so did the Islamic extremists, white supremacists and pornographers (that published the content) which they could then put towards supporting their causes. The backlash saw changes to network advertising to address the issue, but not before a number of the world's major brands – including Coca-Cola, PepsiCo, Wal-Mart, Starbucks and General Motors – announced that they were withdrawing from programmatic advertising. Subsequent action by the networks has not fully addressed this problem.

Do it yourself

One way to beat the ad fraudsters is to keep advertising in-house and keep it small. The majority of the problems described above only occur when third parties (e.g. agencies) get involved, so developing their own ad campaigns on Google and Facebook gives marketers greater control. And the best tips are these: for search ads on Google, turn off the *search partners* options and for Facebook ads, turn off the *audience network* option. This will keep the ads on those platforms and stops them being spread around the web – which is where most of the fraud takes place.

Further reading

For additional content and links to articles and stories that supplement this chapter, go to its web page on www.AlanCharlesworth.com/AEDM.

References

Burke, M., Hornoff, A., Nilsen, E. and Gorman, N. (December 2005) *High-Cost Banner Blindness: Ads Increase Perceived Workload, Hinder Visual Search, and Are Forgotten.* ACM Transactions on Computer-Human Interaction. Volume 12, Issue 4, pp. 423–445.

Frisch, K. (2020) Historic Ad Fraud At Uber with Kevin Frisch. Interview with Alan Hart. Feb. 12, 2020. Marketing Today. Available at: https://www.alistdaily.com/lifestyle/kevin-frisch-uber-ad-fraud/

Kantar (2019) *DIMENSION 2019.* Available at: https://www.kantarmedia.com/dimension/en

Ofcom (2018) *Adults' Media Use and Attitudes Report.* Available at: https://www.ofcom.org.uk/__data/assets/pdf_file/0011/113222/Adults-Media-Use-and-Attitudes-Report-2018.pdf.

Wordstream (2019) *Google Ads Benchmarks for Your Industry* [Updated]. Available at: https://www.wordstream.com/blog/ws/2016/02/29/google-adwords-industry-benchmarks.

7 Email marketing

Essential summary

Despite common misapprehensions – usually prompted by whatever is the latest fad in digital marketing – the death of email as an effective medium for marketing communication is far from certain. This chapter considers three distinct uses of email for the digital marketer. First is the use of email to deliver direct marketing promotions which, unlike marketing on social media, can have clearly defined objectives and measurable return on investment – with the *investment* normally being significantly less for email marketing. It is also a common misconception in digital marketing that email can only be used in a direct marketing context – this is wrong as it ignores the value of *all* email communications as a medium for carrying a marketing message. This concept is investigated before email as the delivery mode for newsletters is examined.

Email as a medium for direct marketing

Direct marketing email campaigns can be broken into six distinct elements. Chronologically, they are:

1 The objectives of the campaign. These will normally be to elicit an action from the recipients. Although sales is most likely to be the desired outcome, often using some kind of inducement, an email campaign might also be used for the likes of encouraging membership of a club, promoting donations to a charity or raising awareness of health concerns.

2   The mailing list. Emails require destination addresses – but to simply send an email to any email address you can find is both poor marketing and potentially illegal. Mailing lists can be developed internally from existing customers and contacts or externally by purchasing lists of email addresses from third-party suppliers who, as a business model, collect email addresses from people who have given their permission to receive emails from organizations with whom they have had no prior communication.

Opting in

Although it also meets legal requirements, getting permission from recipients to send emails to them will result in the most effective campaigns – why would someone not read emails they have, in effect, requested? The best way to get this permission is to have customers take action to confirm their willingness to receive emails. This is known as the *double* opt-in method where the user ticks a box agreeing to emails being sent (*single* opt-in) and is then sent a confirmation email which the recipient must reply to before the opt-in becomes active. Although the double opt-in method reduces take-up rates, it produces databases with the most integrity.

---

3   The content. Because the sender has very little time to impress upon the recipient that (a) the email is not spam, (b) it is relevant to them and (c) they should take the action it promotes, developing email content – words and images – for a successful direct marketing is a specialized task.
4   The landing page. In Chapter 6 the importance of landing pages for ads was stressed. Given that direct marketing emails are essentially *personal* adverts, they are equally important for emails and so everything on landing pages in Chapter 6 is equally relevant here.
5   Test. To ensure that both content and technology is effective, tests should be made of both by sending sample emails. Test variants for content might include such variables as subject lines, colour combinations or different calls-to-action. Technology would include such things as how well the email downloads on various email client servers and screen sizes.
6   Send. Although technology makes this the easiest part of the process, consideration must be given to the time and day they should be dispatched. These decisions are normally based on previous

campaign results – though they could be experimented on as part of the testing process.

7 A final element is to assess the results of the campaign based on the metric identified in the objectives.

Many surveys support the argument for email having an effective role to play in digital marketing. These include:

- Email is the most common activity undertaken online (Perrin, 2020).
- Email is second only to websites for B2B buyers' preferred engagement channel (Marketo, 2018).
- Email topped all other *marketing* methods that influenced millennials' purchases (MarketingCharts and YouGov, 2019).
- Email is the preferred form of communication to resolve issues for 46 per cent of e-commerce site users – sadly, only 26 per cent of sites provide an email address (Sykes Enterprises, 2019).

Email as a medium for marketing messages

Often neglected as a marketing tool, this is the use of email for marketing purposes where the email is *not a direct marketing* message. Because they are often part of a customer's purchase process they are often referred to as *transactional emails* – and to a lesser degree *triggered emails* because they are often automated responses to a customer action. Examples include:

- Welcome messages to new customers can simply say 'hello' but can also include a generic marketing message or a promotion that is specific offer.
- Order, shipping or delivery confirmations are standard now but are also an opportunity to thank the customer for their business and develop a relationship.
- Reservation reminders or status updates – particularly relevant in service industries – can add to the product experience long before the customer samples it.

Perhaps because automated emails are computer generated, the task of developing them it is often left to IT staff or whichever email service provider (ESP) might be used. This is not good practice – according to research by SparkPost (2020) around a third of these marketing messages are written by staff in technical roles who lack the necessary training and skills to write marketing copy. The same SparkPost report found that getting the *tone of voice* right in these emails is essential – something *non-marketers* are unlikely to achieve.

However, not just transactional emails, but *all* out-going emails should be considered for their marketing value – even those that have no overt marketing purpose. Those sent by human resources (e.g. to a prospective employee), finance (an invoice reminder) or procurement (a purchase order) represent the organization as a brand.

Online newsletters

Included in this chapter because they are delivered as *extended* emails these are based on the traditional hard-copy newsletter. The electronically delivered periodic newsletter is a practice – like others in business environments – that seems to drift in and out of fashion. The expansion of social media saw a dip in newsletters' popularity, but the widening availability of so many subjects and sources of information on a variety of social media platforms has led to the contemporary newsletter making a comeback. Distributed on a daily, weekly or monthly basis the editors of subject-specific newsletters do the extensive tracking of events, stories and articles on behalf of the recipient and list only that information they feel will be of interest – saving the reader time in following several social media platforms, or taking the chance of missing something of interest. Newsletters from organizations or brands can use the medium to target messages at self-segmenting audiences, with users being more likely to read something in their email inbox than a message on a social media platform. Indeed, there is an argument that the *requested* – opted-in – newsletter is actually a delivered blog – which makes newsletters more akin to *personal* social media than email. For newsletters, one issue is paramount in their use: the content must appeal to those who have subscribed to receive it. In much the same way as content for the organization's web presence should be developed *properly*, so too must that which is to be distributed to interested parties who have requested it. For the organization that is sending its own *our–company* newsletter *to customers*, developing content is problematic – not only finding interesting subjects, but its writing also. Even if the newsletter is to be little more than a series of links to articles on other sites – with reviews or comments added – those articles must be sourced, read and the comments written; all of which takes time and expertise. However, done correctly, newsletters can work in both B2C and B2B markets.

Further reading

For additional content and links to articles and stories that supplement this chapter, go to its web page on www.AlanCharlesworth.com/AEDM.

References

MarketingCharts and YouGov (2019) *US Purchase Influencers Report 2019.* MarketingCharts.com. Available at: https://www.marketingcharts.com/purchase-influence-report-2019.

Marketo (2018) *The State of Engagement.* Available at: https://www.marketo.com/analyst-and-other-reports/the-state-of-engagement/.

Perrin, N. (2020) *Search in 2020.* eMarketer. Available at: https://www.emarketer.com/content/mobile-search-ad-performance-plays-catch-up.

SparkPost (2020) *Transactional Email Benchmark Report.* Available at: https://www.sparkpost.com/blog/announcing-sparkpost-2020-transactional-email-benchmark-report/.

Sykes Enterprises (2019) *Ecommerce Contact Ratings 2019.* Sykes Enterprises. Available at: https://www.sykes.com/retail/ecommerce-contact-ratings-2019/.

8 Marketing on social media

Essential summary

This chapter starts by considering the difference between social media marketing and marketing on social media as well as what marketing on social media is *not* before considering the key elements of the subject, namely, blogging, networking, sharing and communities, social customer service and support. The remainder of this chapter covers various elements of *strategic* marketing on social media. These start with the objectives and move on to ownership management and implementation. The limitations of marketing on social media are then considered – these include brand followers, rates of engagement, trust and return on investment.

What's in a name?

This chapter carries the title *Marketing on Social Media*, which is at odds with the majority of other sources that use – perhaps simply by habit – *social media marketing* to describe the practice. In its early days, marketers perceived social media purely as a platform for engaging with customers in a social environment, and so to refer to it as *social media marketing* was apt. However, although *engagement* can still be a marketing objective, social media platforms now carry or host marketing messages (e.g. adverts, content marketing and retail listings) and are used for after sales support – all of which are contradictory to the original concept of social engagement. Ultimately, the title used is largely irrelevant, but perhaps by the end of this chapter, readers will accept *marketing on social media* as being a better description of what the practice consists.

Commercial social media?

Like some of the fads and trends in Chapter 1, the term *social commerce* – also known as *social shopping* – has been bandied about as e-commerce on social media platforms. This is something of a misnomer as products are rarely purchased on the platform but follow a link to the seller's website – the concept being more that a potential buyer might use social media for *window shopping.*

If we consider social media to be for social activities *and* business – perhaps we should refer to the latter as *commercial* social media?

What marketing on social media is not

It is important to make clear that *social media* and *marketing on social media* are *not* the same thing. For a whole host of reasons, marketing on social media is misunderstood by practitioners, commentators, writers and students alike. A significant aspect of that misunderstanding comes from what marketing on social media is *not.* It is *not* ...

1 Social media. People using – for example – Facebook are doing so for social intercourse. It does not mean they are all engaging with any marketing performed on that platform.
2 Marketing if a person tells their friends – via social media – about the excellence of a product or service. Apparently, 96 per cent of people *talking* about a brand online do not follow that brand (Windels, 2015).
3 The panacea to all the business and marketing problems, ailments and issues for every organization, brand and product.
4 Free. Social platforms might make no charge (for now) for hosting marketing messages, but those messages must be developed and delivered by people – or software – paid for by the organization.
5 Advertising on social media platforms. This is *advertising* (see Chapter 6).

Social media is about *sharing, relationships* and *engaging in communities* and *networks.* Therefore, marketing on social media must also reflect these characteristics. However, much of what is currently presented as *social media marketing* has nothing to do with *sharing, relationships* and *engaging in communities* and *networks.* Most organizations now

	Customized message	Broadcast message
Profile-based	**Relationship** (social media marketing) Allows marketers to connect, communicate and build relationships with social media messages that are not *promotional* in nature.	**Self-Media** (marketing on social media) Allows marketers to broadcast their promotional messages (e.g. discount offers) to followers (existing customers) as social media content that can be acted upon, liked, followed and forwarded by the target audience. This includes presences on social media platforms that will respond to both external and internal search facilities.
Content-based	**Service** (marketing on social media) Allows marketers to provide answers, advice and help, most commonly as a form of after-sales or customer support service.	**Creative outlet** (advertising on social media) Allows marketers to share their product and brand information— including promotions—with a wider audience of potential customers using programmatic advertising that targets user data.

Figure 8.1 Marketing on social media.

use social media platforms as *broadcast* media for content, news or adverts that is *pushed* out to the general public – the reverse of the ethos of social media. Therefore, marketing on social media is made up of social media marketing (the engagement element) and social broadcast (the non-engagement element). In this context, advertising on social media might be considered to be part of marketing on social media – but it is still better identified as *advertising*. This concept is illustrated in Figure 8.1, a matrix of marketing on social media (adopted by the author from Zhu and Chen, 2015).

Blogging

Along with message boards, blogs were perhaps the original *digital* social media – though social media itself can be traced back over

2000 years (Standage, 2013) with the term *weblog* being first used in 1997 – it being truncated to *blog* a couple of years later. Since that time – and encouraged by the easy (and free) availability of *blogger* sites (e.g. blogger.com) – blogs developed from being more akin to personal journals to mini websites based around the thoughts or interests of the writer. However, the proliferation of alternative modes of social media platforms resulted in blogging losing popularity as the century entered its second decade. Indeed, the way that the likes of Facebook and Twitter are employed by some people actually resembles *mini* blogging. Ironically, the abundance of social media platforms has stimulated *marketing* blogging returning to favour for *niche* writers and publishers who have a following that is willing to put a little effort into reading what he or she has to say – rather than simply checking on Twitter, for example. However, these commercial bloggers are likely to be promoting themselves as a brand (rather than that of their employers) using the blog to put forward their opinions. These views are usually outspoken – which follows the ethos of the early bloggers. These blogs are also more like mini-articles with word counts that far exceed the limits imposed by some social media platforms. However, in an example of multi-platform digital marketing, bloggers will normally have a Twitter account which they use to promote their latest blog entry. In a further example of multi-media social marketing, a blog's content might be reproduced verbally and presented a podcast or on a video – a *vlog*.

Social media: networking, sharing and communities

From its early days through to a time when what is now recognized as social media (let's say the late 2000s after the birth of Facebook and Twitter and when smartphone ownership became commonplace) the different platforms (some now defunct, do any readers remember MySpace – it was the Facebook of its day) served a different purpose for its users. These were loosely classed as *networks* (where you chatted with friends), *sharing* (where you passed on messages) and *virtual communities* (where people with a common interest or hobby gathered). However, brought about by the rise of a few giant brands, the fall of others and diversity by those giants, this is no longer the case – with just about every platform meeting multiple customer needs. If desired, users can network, share and be part of a community on Facebook, Twitter or Instagram, for example – though smaller, niche platforms will always have a role.

So it was that when marketing on social media first gained in popularly it was common practice to segment the different platforms into different marketing purposes or objectives – Twitter for short messages (140 characters back then) and Facebook for longer *engagement* conversations.

With a small number of exceptions, however, that has changed. As with the *social* users, the same platform can be used for multiple marketing purposes – though, as with social, niche platforms can still serve a marketing purpose. It is also the case that some platforms have become more associated with certain types of marketing – Instagram's image-based format appealing to the sale of attire for example, and YouTube for promotions using video. This is, perhaps, not so much due to the platforms themselves, but the way they have been embraced by the users.

Overriding these issues is the topic introduced in Chapter 6 and reinforced at the beginning of this one. Whilst the various platforms can be used by marketers for different approaches for engagement with consumers, all can be used to carry adverts. The nature of each social media platform lends them to targeted advertising. For example:

- YouTube – the video ad that runs before or during videos.
- Twitter – the punchy text and image ad that appears between posts in the user's timeline
- Facebook – display ads at the side of community discussion groups.
- Instagram – ads that are pictures of products being offered for sale

With all of these, the ads can be associated with either the user or the content of the pages – or both.

They come and they go

Although the likes of Facebook, Twitter and Instagram rule the roost at the moment, it was not always so. MySpace, for example, was number one for some time but is now nowhere and Vine was destined for greatness, but it disappeared almost as fast as it emerged. As this chapter is being written (March 2020) TikTok (formerly musical.ly) is the hot new social media platform. It is already massively popular with its users, but there are no real marketing opportunities within it. However, ads are in beta testing – so by the time this book is published expect an ad between just about every song, dance and karaoke performance.

It is worth reminding readers at this point that the sole income of the social media platforms is from hosting adverts – so no matter how user-friendly the social element of the site appears to be, it is the ads that will – have to – carry most prominence. Diversity of income is a driver of many social media brands' initiatives to expand their offering to the public. In this perspective, western companies look with envy at the massive Chinese brands Weibo and WeChat. Although dubbed *social media*, these sites go far beyond offering social services, the nature of their use being more like portals to the Internet, that is the start point of *all* activities on the web – including search and shopping. Facebook have previously stated that this was the aim of the platform – around the same time as they launched the notion of f-commerce – but despite the power of the company they have failed to change westerners' web surfing habits.

Did you know that it is against WhatsApp's terms of service to use the platform for any kind of non-personal (i.e. commercial) use – making it not GDPR-compliant.

Social customer service and support

The popularity of social media platforms, combined with the near ubiquity of smartphones on which to access them, opened up to the marketer the potential for consumer service and support to be delivered online. Though inter-related, service and support on social media can be broken into two elements – *proactive* and *reactive*.

Aimed at improving the customer experience, *proactive* service and support is the use of social media platforms to deliver facilities or actions as part of the overall package offered to the customer when they make a purchase and hence enhancing their use or enjoyment of the purchased product. This could include things such as installation advice (including videos), tips on how best to use the product or operating guidance. Proactive support is well suited to *public* social media platforms as other customers – and potential customers – can see the conversations between the organization and consumers.

Better described as *after-sales* service and support, the reactive option of service and support is delivered in response to customers' requests, queries or complaints. In other words, the customer experience (the proactive aspect of service and support) has failed and the customer is coming to the organization via social media for support, or – more likely – help or recompense.

Social dichotomy

When companies that are online were asked, 80 per cent of respondents said that they deliver *exceptional* social media customer service.

Unfortunately, when their customers were asked, they thought that only eight per cent said that they agree (Mangles, 2018).

Although it is common for organizations to use the likes of Facebook and Twitter in this way, there is a reasonable argument that even with a strong social media team and organizational ethos interactions with dissatisfied customers are best conducted out of the public eye of social media platforms. Therefore, although conversations can be opened on a public space, responses are best kept in one-to-one environments such as the so-called *dark social* (email, the personal massage facility on a social media platform or a messaging app) or good old-fashioned telephone.

Although it is one with limited application, there is a third option; the use of social media for peer-to-peer support. The model is that the organization sets up a support page on a social media platform and then invites other customers to respond to – and answer – questions and issues raised by their peers. This can help create a sense of community amongst customers and create discussion from which the organization might benefit (solutions or suggestions might help improve existing products or the development of new products). Although staff are needed to monitor the discussions so that they can step in if peers' responses are not forthcoming or incorrect answers are supplied, the model makes possible significant savings in resources so that more expensive call centres or helpdesks are not required.

Strategic marketing on social media

There are two key issues to address with regard to engaging in marketing on social media; (1) the objectives and (2) its management and implementation.

Objectives

There are a number of considerations for the organization before determining any strategic marketing on social media objectives, namely:

1 Is it what our customers expect from us? If the answer to this question is 'yes', then the organization should be active in social media.
2 Is social media worth the effort? Is there any ROI, if not how much is the loss?
3 Is it *right* for the organization? If the nature of the product, brand or organization doesn't generate passion or interest, then the very culture of the organization might disqualify it from effective participation.
4 Does it fit in with our other marketing efforts – both offline and online?
5 What elements of social media are suitable for our objectives?

A further objective that has little to do with customer engagement is that of achieving a listing on search engine listings (as covered in Chapter 2). However, SERP success is normally a by-product of an effective social media strategy rather than the reason for it. To have a social media page listed in a search for the organization, brand or product then that page must be active – the SERP usually shows the latest posting – the search engines recognizing a *fabricated* social media presence.

Ownership, management and implementation

Marketing on social media needs to be an organization-wide initiative, but to be effective it must have a single point of *ownership*. However, if strategic responsibility lies within the marketing department, it is not necessarily where *operational* issues take place. Marketing content for social media is best developed and delivered by staff that have the ability to write effectively and with the necessary skills, training and education to best represent the product, brand or organization. Although some marketers will have the ability, it is more likely that the necessary skills are found in the public relations (PR) department where the staff will have either journalistic backgrounds or they have studied journalistic skills as part of a public relations-based education programme. However, it is often the case that PR staff lack the relevant marketing education and/or experience to see the role *social* plays in the organization's wider strategic marketing; hence, the *ownership* issue.

Limitations of marketing on social media

The value to organizations, brands and products of marketing on social media is questioned by many. Key problematic issues include why people follow a brand, trust and return on investment.

Brand followers

Social media marketing evangelists – often those selling related services – quote figures about social media use (*everybody* on the planet, it would seem) and make statements like 'social media is the place that everyone goes to when they want to connect with organizations'. Doubters respond by pointing out that everyone sees the sky everyday – but that does not make it the best place to host marketing messages. Similarly, social media might be the place everyone goes *if they wish to connect* with organizations, but not every customer *wants* to connect. Even a quick glance around any kitchen will reveal a glut of products from toaster to bread, plates to rice and chairs to herbs that we have no reason to connect with their manufacturers, processors or even retailers. Although pure numbers of followers an organization has might be impressive, they should be set against numbers of customers. In 2016 Kumar et al. found that the percentage of a firm's customers that participate in their social media sites ranged from 1.00 per cent to 7.35 per cent, with an average of 3.7 per cent. Newer research is not readily available, but there is no reason to suspect that similar research conducted now would yield a wide variation to these numbers. Exceptions obviously exist, but the law of averages suggests that there must be many organizations that are closer to the 1.00 per cent mark. It is hard to think of any other marketing activity that would be continued if such a small proportion of its customer base was reached by a marketing message. The reasons why people follow a brand on social media as found in the results of research by Sprout Social (2020), which is representative of similar surveys – the results are shown in Figure 8.2.

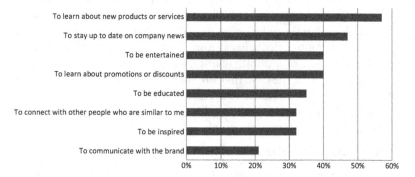

Figure 8.2 Why consumers follow brands on social media (Sprout Social, 2020).

These figures provide interesting reading for social media marketers. That around half seek some kind of entertainment suggests the social media presences offer videos or the like (e.g. on YouTube), and so *engagement* is minimal. However, that 50 per cent want to learn about new products and services is encouraging to those organizations that have a stream of new products for the market. That promotions and discounts account for 38 per cent is good news for those companies that offer such enticements, but not so good for organizations seeking engagement (a Tweet that says '25% off today' is an advert not an engagement). The responses on inspiration, education and connecting with people suggest that that some of the brands being followed are not overtly commercial (e.g. retailers) but offer some kind of social support – a news outlet, not-for-profit, community or celebrity presence, for example. Sadly, Sprout Social does not disclose their definition of *brand* for this research. The results suggest that respondents have used a wide interpretation, which may impact any strategic decisions based on them. For example, followers of Selena Gomez might seek inspiration and to connect with fellow fans of the American singer – which is very different if you are selling white goods or manufacturing components.

Sprout Social's research also investigated why people un-follow a brand, the results are shown in Figure 8.3. Other than poor customer service – the data does not state so specifically, but it would be reasonable to assume that poor offline service results in online rejection – the reasons would appear to be a failure to meet expectations of following

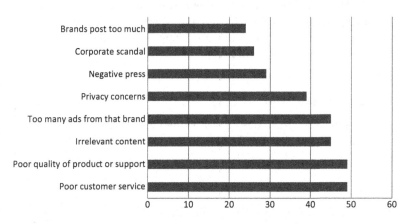

Figure 8.3 Why consumers un-follow brands on social media (Sprout Social, 2020).

in the first place. Findings of this kind also support the notion that most followers are already *customers* of the brands they follow. Why, for example, would nearly 160 million people (as of February 2020) follow Selena Gomez on Instagram if they did not like her, her music and her thoughts on life? (i.e. they had bought into the *brand* that is Selena Gomez). Similarly, why would anyone *like* Starbucks if they hadn't sampled the products of the ubiquitous coffee provider?

This is significant for marketers when considering their marketing objectives for social media campaigns. Whilst existing customers might be ripe for social engagement, having a presence on social media does not appear to be an effective way to attract new customers. Note that it has not been proven conclusively either way that followers of a brand will spend more money with that brand than someone who is not following it. It is an issue of *cause* and *effect* – do followers spend more because they are followers or are they followers because they spend more?

Rates of engagement

For the majority of organizations, the *stated* objective of using social media as a platform for marketing is to *engage* with customers. Research from Socialbakers (2020) considered the industries that fare best in interactions on Facebook and Instagram brand pages around the world. These are shown in Figure 8.4. Whilst the results are good news for e-commerce and fashion, that is not the case for the other industries identified. This is particularly the case for the many hundreds of industries that are included in 'others'. Furthermore, the research revealed that the type of post that generated the *most* engagement on that Instagram (carousels) achieved, on average, only 125 interactions per post. That does not say much for the posts that generated the lowest average number of interactions.

One-way engagement?

As of February 2020, despite following no one and posting zero messages, Apple has 9,582,170 followers on LinkedIn.

Trust on social media

Offline, scepticism of marketing messages abounds – but on social media scepticism has moved on to distrust. Research from YouGov (2019) investigated how much users trust commercial postings from

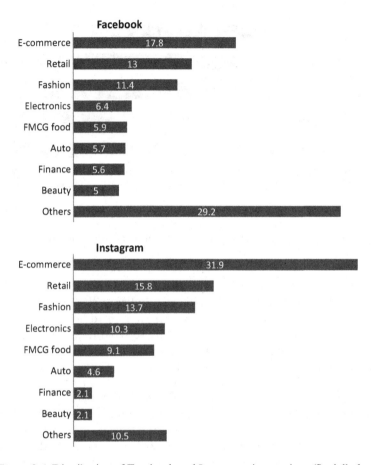

Figure 8.4 Distribution of Facebook and Instagram interactions (Socialbakers, 2020).

celebrities, influencers and business leaders on social media platforms by comparing them to friends and family. The results – shown in Figure 8.5 – are not encouraging for marketers with companies, influencers and celebrities generally considered to be *not at all honest*.

Return on investment (ROI)

If marketing on social media is to be adopted, the organization must set metrics upon which ROI will be judged. And therein lays the key

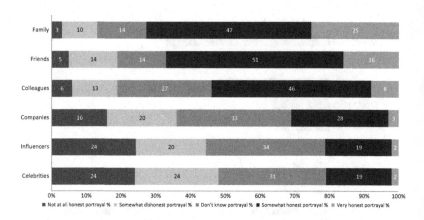

Figure 8.5 Users' perceptions of honesty on social media (YouGov, 2019).

problem: *what do we measure?* Early social media marketers followed conventional wisdom and assumed that audience size was the most important measure of success, and so they counted how many *fans, followers, friends* or *likes* (now commonly referred to as being *vanity* metrics as they mean more to managers than the organization's marketing efforts) they could amass. This meant that they concentrated more on building these metrics – usually by tactics that owed more to traditional marketing than they did to social media marketing. Furthermore, some of the followers being counted were (and still to a lesser degree still are) fake followers being *bought* – often thousands for only a few dollars. However, the value of having a thousand or even a million followers with no proof that they were increasing sales or brand value was questioned by some in the industry. One of the doubters was Irfan Kamal (Senior Vice President, Digital/Social Strategy at Ogilvy & Mather) who in 2011 made the point that:

> … we need to measure metrics that are related to business value. Does social media change brand perception? Does it increase consideration? Does it drive actual sales for the brand? What often gets measured instead are … diagnostic or optimization metrics – the number of Facebook fans, the Twitter follower base, the size of a group or a message board or a LinkedIn group. All the metrics that are easily visible are the ones that end up getting measured most

often. The problem is that it's unclear whether there is a direct relationship between these metrics and genuine business value.

Unfortunately, Kamal's comments – and their inferences – are still ignored by many organizations. Perhaps the reluctance to establish KPIs that can be usefully analyzed is they are difficult to identify. Therefore, identifying desired outcomes for strategic social campaigns is a necessity – and it must be better that the current common practice of (a) performing some – often expensive – marketing on social media, (b) collecting some data and then (c) trying to reconcile the two. Basic *measurable* metrics might include any or all of the following.

- Increase engagement through *likes* and *followers?* Were posts forwarded or re-*tweeted*.
- Increase visitors to the organization's own website through clicks from social media platforms.
- Increase brand awareness in key target markets.
- Increase brand recognition.
- Increase the product and/or brand's market share.

Should the social marketer be able to identify suitable objectives, a variety of tools for social media data gathering and analysis are available from numerous software vendors, including the following.

- Social media monitoring tools that monitor the various platforms for posts, tweets, conversations or even hashtags that are relevant to the product, brand or organization.
- Social site-specific tools, commonly provided by the platform's publishers with more complex versions from specialist vendors.
- Influencer identification tools which are used to identify those social influencers that the product, brand or organization might wish to engage with.

The capability of these products has expanded significantly due to a combination of social media adoption, client needs and advances in technology Charlesworth (2017).

Further reading

For additional content and links to articles and stories that supplement this chapter, go to its web page on www.AlanCharlesworth.com/AEDM.

References

Charlesworth, A. (2017) *Marketing on Social Media – Marketing Panacea or the Emperor's New Digital Clothes?* Business Expert Press. New York.

Kumar, A., Bezawada, R., Rishika, R., Janakiraman, R., and Kannan, P. K. (January 2016) *From Social to Sale: The Effects of Firm-Generated Content in Social Media on Customer Behavior.* Journal of Marketing. ISSN: 0022–2429 (print). Volume 80, pp. 7–25.

Mangles, C. (2018) *The Rise of Social Media Customer Care.* Smart Insights. Available at: https://www.smartinsights.com/customer-relationship-management/customer-service-and-support/rise-social-media-customer-care/.

Socialbakers (2020) *Instagram vs. Facebook Report.* Available at: https://www.socialbakers.com/social-media-content/studies/instagram-vs-facebook-report-key-trends-you-need-to-know.

Sprout Social (2020) *Sprout Social Index Edition XVI.* Available at: https://media.sproutsocial.com/uploads/2020-Sprout-Social-Index-Above-and-Beyond.pdf

Standage, T. (2013) *Writing on the Wall.* Bloomsbury.

Windels, J. (2015) *Marketing: Dark Matter, Social Media and the Number 96.* Brandwatch. Available at: https://www.brandwatch.com/blog/marketing-dark-matter-social-media-and-the-number-96/.

YouGov (2019) *YouGov Analysis of Honesty and Social Media.* Available online at; https://yougov.co.uk/topics/resources/articles-reports/2019/10/30/honesty-and-social-media.

Zhu, Y-Q. and Chen, H-G. (May–June 2015) *Social Media and Human Need Satisfaction: Implications for Social Media Marketing.* Business Horizons. Volume 58, Issue 3, pp. 335–345.

9 Metrics and analytics

Essential summary

The final chapter starts by establishing the basics of the subject by defining metrics, analytics, data gathering and the skills required in the practice of data analytics. Consideration is then given to what is being measured with attention given to websites, advertising, email and social media. The focus then switches to the limitations of online data with questions being raised with regard to the right data being collected, how much of the Internet is fake and the problems with metrics.

The basics

Before moving forward, it is necessary for the digital marketer to be aware of the key elements of the subject area. A good place to start is with what metrics and analytics are – and they are *not* the same thing.

Metrics

Sometimes referred to as *e*-metrics when applied online – metrics are standards of measurement. Basic *business* metrics include things such as sales units, sales revenue, net profit margin and gross margin. Online marketing metrics take in demographics associated with website visitors such as where in the world they live, their gender and their age, how long they stay on the site and if they buy anything. Because these metrics serve to indicate how well (or badly) the business is performing, they are often referred to as indicators with the most important being referred to as *key performance indicators* (KPIs).

Analytics

Analytics seek patterns in the data gathered as metrics that can be used in the future and so are used to create models which can – for example – help understand, monitor and predict customer behaviour. For this reason, analytics is also referred to as *modelling* or *forecasting*. Taking into consideration any statistics created by variables within the data has also resulted in the term *statistical analysis* being used.

Attribution

Closely related to both metrics *and* analytics – specifically, the measurement of the success or failure of marketing strategies and tactics – is which element of marketing is attributed with achieving the required outcome. Attribution is another element of digital marketing that has its origins in offline marketing – specifically, *promotion* and *advertising*. The original notion comes from social psychology where *attribution* refers to an individual's explanation of the causes of behaviour and events, a model known as *attribution theory* – the same name being applied when it was adopted by business. As far as marketing is concerned, attribution is identifying what – if any – aspects of marketing prompted someone to take the action desired by the marketer. Generally, this would be to buy a product, but it can be other things such as contribute to a charity or vote for a candidate.

When first used in digital marketing the aim was to determine the online location of where the customer made the final *click* to arrive on the website where a purchase was made – and so became known as *last click attribution*. Originally a straight fight between advertising and search engine optimization, this fragmented when advertising became more complex and was divided into *network, search* and *native*. Although the marketers were seeking to use the data to help build an understanding of customer buyer behaviour, they also wanted to know what marketing efforts were working, what wasn't and which gave the best return on investment. Unfortunately, rivalry between the digital marketing factions took hold – with prestige, budget allocations (and so, jobs) being the prize for bringing about the *last click*. The problem is, however, that although someone might, for example, have searched for a generic product (e.g. washing machine), which triggered personalized ads which the customer saw over the next few days – and prompted them to visit the website of a prominent retailer. However, it was only when they had read other customers' reviews on that site that they made the purchase, and so it is the retailer's review page that takes the rewards of being the *last click*. Viewed objectively, this is a nonsensically conclusion. And this is a relatively simple example. For a more complex product or service, the buying process will be longer, and use more channels. Online alone, as well as the seller's own web and social media sites, third-party websites such as price comparison sites, review sites and blogs might play a part in the user coming to a buying conclusion. In addition, there is the mass of offline marketing – so-called *multichannel* marketing – any element of which (e.g. TV ads) might have contributed to that *last click* being made. Worse still for the digital marketer is that after being convinced by a whole host of online marketing the customer might go into a physical store to make the purchase, so there is no *last click*. Furthermore, the buying process might have taken place over several months – or even years.

As well as the final click, equally important to the marketer is iden-tifying which element might have caused the potential buyer to reject the product. This may have been because they simply decided that the product was not for them. However, it could have been as a result of poor marketing. Even worse, after *coaxing* a potential customer down the purchase funnel with a series of well-executed marketing tactics, if the last element is poorly executed then the customer might make their last click onto a competitor's website. Alternatives to the final link in the chain getting 100 per cent of the credit include; reversing the model and awarding all of the credit to the *first* click; *time decay* where the last link takes the most credit and each other link takes less; *position based* where the first and last links take equally high credit with other links sharing the remainder or linear where every link takes equal credit. Another option is the *post last* click. This involves the marketer ignoring how the customer got to the sales website and concentrating on the successful completion of a sale through the creation of an *excel-lent* customer experience whilst they are on the website.

Naturally, none of these can be seen as being ideal for every product or brand in every industry or market. Therefore, the marketer must identify what is best for their organization, brand or product. How-ever, that is not easy, and unsurprisingly there is general consensus that the *perfect* attribution model does not exist.

Data gathering (data mining)

Mined data has three sources, they are:

1   First-party data is that which is gathered *by* the organization *for* the organization and as such is the most authoritative and important. It will come from all points of contact between the

organization and the customer and is generally transactional and behavioural.

2   Second-party data is where organizations use the first-party data of another organization – a supplier of bespoke kitchens using that of a white goods manufacturer, for example.

3   Third-party data is aggregated by organizations for whom the practice is a business (sometimes called the Data-as-a-Service – DaaS – industry). Where First-party data is specific, third party can provide context and relevance. It is generally gathered via third-party cookies deposited on users' devices by a myriad of websites.

Analytic skills

There is a common assumption amongst digital marketers that metrics and analytics are all equations, algorithms and hard maths – this is no longer the case. However, the necessary skills are still in short supply – those skill sets can be broken into three key areas:

1   Information technology/computer science – to collect (mine) the data and present it in *visual* or *descriptive* formats such as charts, graphs and tables (dashboards) that are easily understood. Software is the enabler in this skill set.

2   Data analytics/science – to work with the data and turn it into information by developing custom dashboards, analyzing tests and results. This is where the maths comes in.

3   Marketing – to take the information and evaluate it in terms of business and marketing, so determining the *why* of the numbers and how that information can be used in the development of future tactics and strategies. As much of this is subjective, it adds a degree of *art* to the *science*.

These do not have to be three separate people or teams – there are individuals out there who can do all three. However, they are few in number – that the first two skills are science based and the latter art is perhaps the main reason for this being the case. For major organizations, online-only traders and agencies that specialize in analytics, having skills in the three areas is essential. However, for the smaller enterprise, software has come to the aid of marketers. Led by Google (who provide more data than the majority of digital marketers will ever need), the *science* part of the discipline is completed in the background and presented to the marketers in easy-to-read *dashboards* of information. Some dashboards are fairly basic and others more complex. There are also analytic dashboard developers, some who use propriety data and others who develop a personalized dashboard from Google data. Worth noting is that at this level, so common is the use of this supportive software that when marketers say they are *doing analytics* they are most likely referring to using a specific commercial platform and its dashboard.

Finally, it is worth reminding readers that despite the term analytics being used in describing the dashboard software, the data itself has not been analyzed, it has been *sorted*. Knowing, for example, that 47 per cent of visitors to a website arrive via a search engine is not *analysis*. Analysis is investigating *why* that might be the case. Is it a positive or negative? If it's positive, how might it be taken advantage of? If it's negative, how can it be corrected? How does it fit in with other results or marketing initiatives? Although other data might help with these answers, effective analysis can only be conducted by people with business and marketing insights.

What help is available?

The two major players in the provision of data metrics and analytics are Google and Adobe. Google analytics are free for a basic package of services with charges for more advanced packages. Users have to pay for licences to use Adobe. Other services offered by Google – ads and SEO for example – are built in to its analytics package, making it an attractive one-stop service. Comparatively, both have advantages and disadvantages, but overall Adobe is mostly used by big firms and agencies (where technical support is available) whilst Google is mostly used by smaller and mid-level organizations or websites.

What is being measured?

Digital communications offer the marketer something never before available – the ability to gather data on every aspect of marketing that is related to the online environment. In the early days – and still today to a limited extent – the ability to gather an almost infinite amount of data was seen as an opportunity not to be ignored. As a result – and this was more often than not driven by technology-providers – vast mountains of data were collected. However, best practice is to gather only that data that (a) can be analyzed, and (b) as a result of that analysis provides information on which decisions can be made. Some of the most commonly identified website metrics and resultant analytics include the following.

- Visitor numbers – more visitors mean more people being exposed to the brand.
- Number of visits by individuals – returning visitors might suggest brand loyalty.
- How deep into the site visitors go – more pages accessed implies an interest in the brand's offerings.
- How long visitors stay on the site – the longer the stay the greater the affiliation might be to the brand ... but it could mean information is difficult to find.
- Conversion rate – the percentage of visitors to the website versus sales achieved or the percentage of visitors to the website who go on to contact the firm versus sales.

Basic *website* metrics made available by Google include:

- Pageviews – the total number of pages viewed.
- Unique pageviews – the number of sessions (user visits) during which the specified page was viewed at least once.
- Average time on page – the average amount of time users spent viewing a specified page.
- Average session duration – the average amount of time users spent on the site in a visit.
- Bounce rate – a *bounce* is a single-page session on a site. The bounce rate is the number of one-page visits divided by the total number of visits.
- Devices – were visitors using a PC or mobile device.
- The geographic location of each visitor to the site.
- Clickstream – a brief section of the visitor's path through the site.

Advertising metrics include:

- How many people clicked through to a landing page from the ad.
- Where they were – geographically.
- What page they were on when the ad was displayed.
- Tracking the user through to a purchase – or rejection.

Generic *email* metrics include such things as:

- Delivery rate – the percentage of sent emails that reach a 'live' inbox.
- Open rate – the percentage of sent emails that are opened by the receiver.
- Clickthrough rate – the percentage of sent emails that are opened and then have an embedded link *clicked.*
- Viral rate – how many opened emails are forwarded to another address.
- Campaign comparison – any of the above measured against metrics from similar previous campaigns.
- The churn rate – the loss of addresses from an email list.

The major *social media* platforms also provide basic metrics, these are shown in Table 9.1.

Limitations of online data

Whilst some digital evangelists point to data as being the answer – or *route* to the answer – of all digital marketing problems, others question aspects of it.

The right data?

Customers are willing to live with having data about them collected and stored, but at the same time they expect that any data gathered on them will be used to provide a better service. The problem comes with organizations collecting data that is rarely useful in improving service. In marketing terms, it offers no value to the customer in return for them agreeing to give data. The result of this is the discord shown by the general public towards the use of their personal data. Furthermore, the

Table 9.1 Metrics provided by the major social media platforms.

Facebook	Twitter
Actions on the page	Number of Tweets made
Page views	How many impressions for each Tweet
Page likes	How many followers
Post reach	How many mentions Tweets get
Post engagement	How many visits to profile page

Note, however, that the value of these social media metrics is questioned by most marketers. Dismissively described as *vanity metrics*, the argument is that their analysis does nothing to help organizations assess any marketing that has been conducted on social media.

data collected – because it is easy to acquire – is behavioural and demo-graphic ... and it is *historical*. It tells how people acted, not how they *will* act. And it suggests *generic* customer buyer behaviour, not that which is relevant to different products. An individual's buyer behaviour towards something that interests them (a new bicycle, for example) will not be the same as that for something that they perceive to be a chore (a new refrigerator). Marketers would be better placed if they concentrated on more customer-specific data – unsurprisingly, this is first-party data. This *psychological* data is context-specific for each customer for the product or products the organization is selling. Some commentators suggest that restrictions on the collection of data imposed by the recent General Data Protection Regulation (GDPR) and California Consumer Privacy Act (CCPA) initiatives will see a move towards the collection of only data that will *genuinely* add value for the customer.

How much of the Internet is fake?

Because they are countable and verifiable, metrics *should* be the most factual element of Internet – they serve to underpin the online advertis-ing which supports social and search platforms allowing users get them for free. They support the digital marketer in arguing that digital is *the* place for marketing to take place. Metrics are, essentially, the user's digital footprint on the web. As with any data collection, there will al-ways be margins of error, the misreading and miscalculation and flawed assumptions. These are not real concerns for the data analyzer – the problem is just how much of digital metrics are fake. That is; deliber-ately – not accidentally – inaccurate. In Chapter 6 the issue of ad fraud was raised – describing how phoney web users were conceived in order to cheat advertisers out of ad expenditure. These phantom users num-ber not in the hundreds or thousands, or even hundreds of thousands, but millions – possibly billions. So, when you read (there are multiple sources) that last year, last month, last week or yesterday X million us-ers surfed the web – how many are real people and how many *fakes*? How many page visits are made by real people and how many by soft-ware-generated robots of some kind?

Problems with metrics

This list is by no means exhaustive, but it will give readers a gist of the issues that are out there.

- By and large, statistics from radio, TV and print media are ac-cepted as being an accurate representation of the number of *people* that listen, watch and read their products – not least because all are subject to third-party auditing. Online metrics represent devices or software, and there is no independent auditing.

- Analytics tools place code on a website so when a browser loads a page, the code places a cookie and records what the user is doing. However, ad blockers prevent the code and so if a blocker is used by the surfer (in their browser) the website does not record them as a visitor. In the UK it is *estimated* – no one *actually* knows – that between 20 and 25 per cent of surfers use ad blockers. That's the surfing behaviour of around a quarter of *real* people on the web who are anonymous to metrics.

- Industry analysts do not agree on a specific number, but it is agreed that many website visitors are not humans, but bots (software applications that runs automated tasks over the Internet). Results from research by bot management company, Distil Networks (2019) suggest that 37.9 per cent of website traffic is bots – a figure that is around the average of estimates from other sources. So, if a website's metrics say it had 1000 visitors, it's likely to be closer to 600.

- Mobile metrics have problems unique to smartphone users in that if the user is on a website and they pass from one transmission tower to another it appears to the metrics as being another user.

- As with other platforms verifiable numbers of fraudulent accounts on Twitter are difficult to come by, though the social media platform admitted to a Securities and Exchange Commission that in 2014 it estimated that 8.5 per cent of its active monthly users were automated accounts. Given the increase in users since then – and the rise in numbers of *influencers* (whose payments are based on numbers of followers) this number appears conservative. Spark-Toro, a business that investigates false followers on Twitter accounts of their clients, state on their website (SparkToro.com) that according to their research 5–30 per cent of all followers on the platform are either bots, spam accounts, inactive users, propaganda or other non-engaged/non-real users.

- Instagram is host to more influencers than any other platform – and so the validity of their followers is critical to marketers. According to a study by research firm Ghost Data for The Information (Albergotti and Kuranda, 2018) Instagram's fake follower count stands at around 9.5 per cent.

- Facebook's problems with fake followers has been well chronicled in the press, not least that in 2016 the social media giant admitted that they had overstated average video view times by 60 to 80 per cent. Remember, advertising fees are based on view times.

Further reading

For additional content and links to articles and stories that supplement this chapter, go to its web page on www.AlanCharlesworth.com/AEDM.

References

Albergotti, R. and Kuranda, S. (2018) *Instagram's Growing Bot Problem*. Available at: https://www.theinformation.com/articles/instagrams-growing-bot-problem.

Distil Networks (2019) *Bad Bot Report 2019: The Bot Arms Race Continues*. Available at: https://resources.distilnetworks.com/white-paper-reports/bad-bot-report-2019.

Index

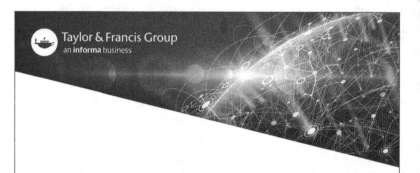

Printed in the United States
by Baker & Taylor Publisher Services